¡MEXICO!

40 ACTIVITIES TO EXPERIENCE MEXICO PAST & PRESENT

Susan Milord

Illustrations by
Michael Kline

WILLIAMSON PUBLISHING • CHARLOTTE, VT

CONTENTS

¡MEXICO!

A WILLIAMSON *KALEIDOSCOPE KIDS*™ BOOK

DEDICATION

For Bob, *por supuesto*

ACKNOWLEDGEMENTS

Many thanks to Professor William Haviland, Jennifer Ingersoll, Marco Nuñez, Brett Whalen, and Lisa Breslof of the American Museum of Natural History, for their valuable contributions and insights.

Williamson Publishing Books by Susan Milord

¡Mexico!

Bird Tales from Near & Far

Tales of the Shimmering Sky

Tales Alive! Ten Multicultural Tales and Activities

Hands Around the World

Adventures in Art

The Kids' Nature Book

Copyright © 1999 by Susan Milord

All rights reserved.

No portion of this book may be reproduced mechanically, electronically, or by any other means including photocopying or on the Internet without written permission of the publisher.

Library of Congress Cataloging-in-Publication Data

Milord, Susan.
  Mexico! : 40 activities to experience Mexico past & present / by Susan Milord.
    p.   cm.
  "A kaleidoscope kids book."
  Includes bibliographical references and index.
  Summary: Discusses the history, language, religion, customs, and daily life of Mexico, using a variety of activities to reinforce the information.
    ISBN 1-885593-22-8 (alk. paper)
    1. Mexico–Juvenile literature.   2. Activity programs in education–Juvenile literature. [1. Mexico.] I. Title.
  F1208.5.M55   1998
   972–dc21   98-34153
               CIP
               AC

Design: **Joseph Lee Design: Joseph Lee, Diane Phillips**
Illustrations: **Michael Kline Illustration**
Kaleidoscope Kids™ Series Editor: **Susan Williamson**
Photography: **Laurie Platt Winfrey, Inc.**
  (Pages: 35, 36, 39, 48, 57, 67, 70, 73, 76)
Printing: **Quebecor Printing, Inc.**

Printed in Canada

Williamson Publishing Co.
P.O. Box 185
Charlotte, Vermont 05445
1-800-234-8791

10 9 8 7 6 5 4 3 2 1

Little Hands®, *Kids Can!*®, and *Tales Alive*® are registered trademarks of Williamson Publishing Company.

Kaleidoscope Kids™ and *Good Times™* are trademarks of Williamson Publishing Company.

MEXICO: WHERE PAST AND PRESENT MEET

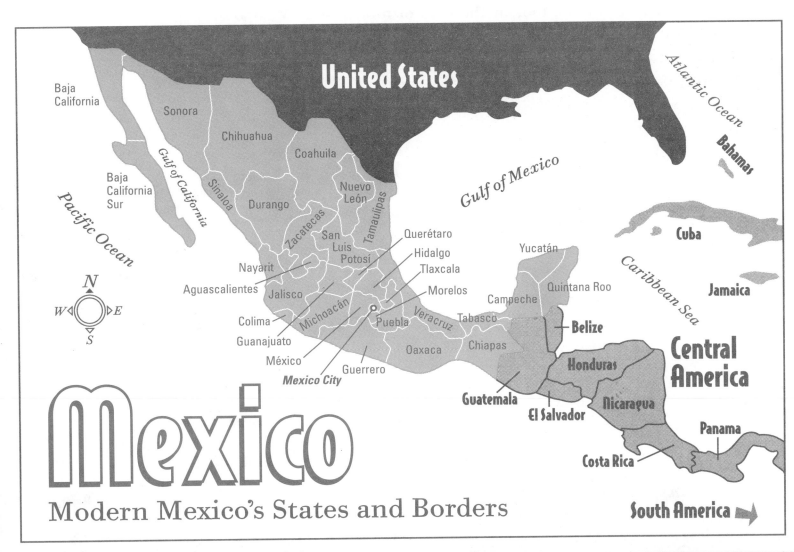

Mexico

Modern Mexico's States and Borders

I magine a place where you can dip your toes in the same salty ocean water your distant ancestors enjoyed; where the earth rumbles and volcanoes spew clouds of steam as they have done for thousands of years; where you can visit tiny villages with life continuing much as it has for centuries; and where you can meet people whose history is like a colorful blanket woven with ancient Indian and rich Spanish traditions. Where is this incredible place? Mexico!

On your time-lapsed journey through Mexico — a country very much a part of the Americas — you'll meet people from times long past and places you may never have heard of. As with any journey, it's best to know the lay of the land and where you are in time. So, look at the map of modern-day Mexico on page 5. Notice its long shape stretching north and south between the

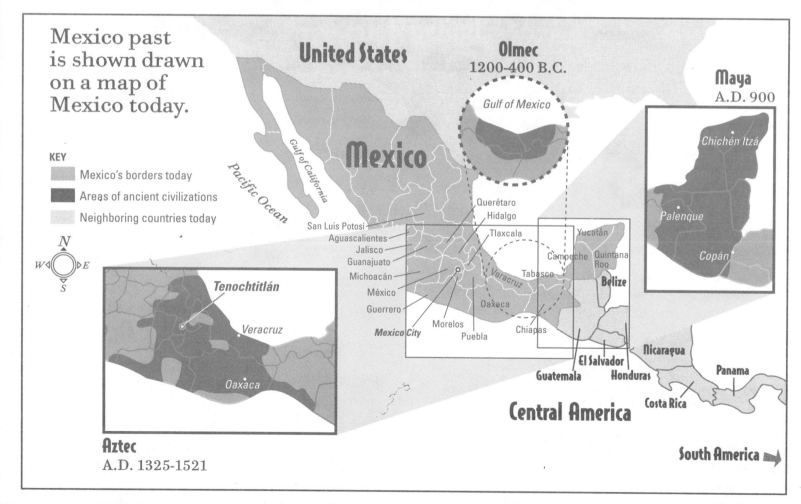

Mexico past is shown drawn on a map of Mexico today.

KEY
- Mexico's borders today
- Areas of ancient civilizations
- Neighboring countries today

United States

Olmec
1200–400 B.C.

Maya
A.D. 900

Gulf of Mexico

Chichén Itzá

Gulf of California

Pacific Ocean

Mexico

Palenque

Copán

Querétaro
Hidalgo
San Luis Potosí
Tlaxcala
Yucatán
Aguascalientes
Jalisco
Campeche
Quintana Roo
Guanajuato
Veracruz
Tabasco
Michoacán
México
Oaxaca
Belize
Guerrero
Mexico City
Morelos
Puebla
Chiapas

Tenochtitlán

Veracruz

Oaxaca

Nicaragua

El Salvador
Panama
Guatemala
Honduras

Costa Rica

Central America

Aztec
A.D. 1325–1521

South America ➡

Pacific Ocean and the Gulf of Mexico, who its neighbors are, and the names of some of its 31 states.

Now, look at the historical map on page 6. Here you see not only the shape of Mexico today and the names of some of its present-day states for reference, but superimposed (drawn over) are the areas where Mexico's ancient civilizations developed. Knowing where these civilizations were founded tells you a lot about the people who live there today, because even all these years later, Mexico draws on traditions, arts, and beliefs of those ancient peoples. Also, on the map below, see the areas to the north annexed (joined) to the United States after the Mexican-American War.

If you turn to page 31, you will find a topographical map that shows Mexico's topography, or its mountains, valleys, plateaus, and large bodies of water. From these you can practically guess why different lifestyles developed, where trade prospered, where today's tourists plan vacations, and where people have been isolated by mountains.

Lastly, turn to page 53. Take a look at the time line, so you can begin to see the changes in the dominant civilizations that ruled Mexico for long periods, because, of course, they each left the mark of their cultures on Mexico, too.

Ah, good! Now we're ready to meet the people, past and present, in earnest!

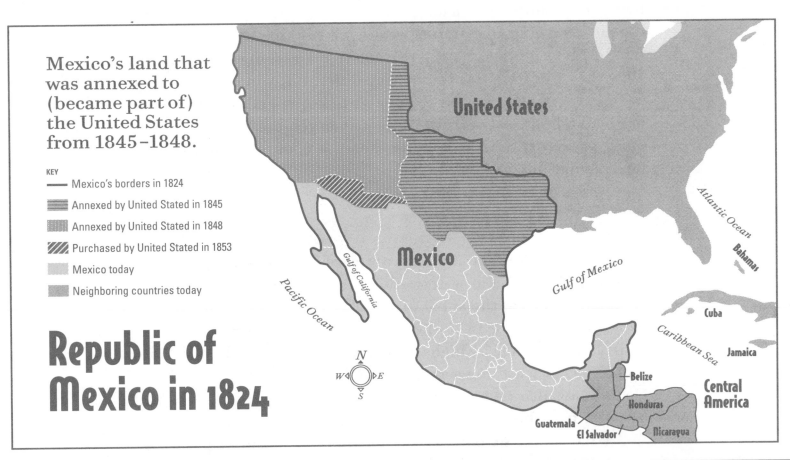

Mexico's land that was annexed to (became part of) the United States from 1845–1848.

KEY
— Mexico's borders in 1824
▦ Annexed by United Stated in 1845
▦ Annexed by United Stated in 1848
▨ Purchased by United Stated in 1853
▦ Mexico today
▦ Neighboring countries today

Republic of Mexico in 1824

United States

Gulf of California

Mexico

Pacific Ocean

Gulf of Mexico

Atlantic Ocean

Bahamas

Cuba

Caribbean Sea

Jamaica

Belize

Central America

Honduras

Guatemala

El Salvador

Nicaragua

N W E S

A Kid Is a Kid Is a Kid...

What's it like to grow up in Mexico? For many kids, growing up is much the same as it is for you. Mexican kids love being with their families. They have favorite foods, favorite television shows, favorite things they like to do with friends. They play games and participate in sports. And, kids are proud of their individual heritage, too.

Kids in Mexico have a unique perspective that comes from living in a country with a long and colorful past. So, whether from the city or country, or from a wealthy, a working class, or a poor family, Mexican children and teens have many things in common. How they live from day to day may differ, but you can bet every kid enjoys playing games, eating *tortillas,* spending time with family, and playing with friends – just as you do! That's because kids, no matter where they live, share a common bond – they love having fun!

THE LIFE OF A CITY KID

Say you live in Mexico City, the capital of Mexico – not only Mexico's largest city, but also the world's. You're very used to the noise of honking horns, the smell of vehicle exhaust, and crowds.

You might live in a one-story house built around a small courtyard protected by high walls to keep the city noise out. Your family has at least one servant, who not only cooks, shops, and cleans, but also looks after you. You learn to garden, or cook, and sew from her.

What about school? Well, you probably attend a parochial

(religious) school run by the Catholic church. Your teachers are priests and nuns, and you wear a school uniform (making it easy to get ready for school each day!). Your school subjects include learning English. If your school is too far to walk to, you take the Metro, the city's subway system.

What kinds of clothes do you wear? Pretty much the same kinds of clothes other kids in North America wear. T-shirts, jeans, and sneakers are the perfect fit all over the world!

Of course, not everyone in Mexico City lives like this. If you are a very poor child, you might live in one of the city's many slums, called "lost cities." You share a one-room house with many family members, possibly including your grandparents, aunts, and uncles. Your house might not have electricity or running water. When times are really tough, you might even beg for food or for any coins passers-by might toss your way.

THE LIFE OF A COUNTRY KID

Suppose you live in the country: How might your life differ from that of a city kid's? For one thing, it's a lot quieter! You live in an adobe (mud brick) house, and your family grows much of its food.

If you're a boy, you probably help your father work the fields with a horse and wooden plow, sowing seeds by hand. If you're a girl, you might spend your time helping your mother cook, clean, and look after your younger brothers and sisters.

Whether you're a boy or a girl, you probably go to school, where you are taught in Spanish, even if it is not the language you and your family speak at home.

In your free time, you play outdoors, perhaps kicking a soccer ball around with your friends. You don't get many opportunities to go to the movies, but you probably watch television.

The pace may be slower in the country than in the city, but there's never any lack of things to do.

Think About It

Hmmm—Where Would I Like to Live?

So, what do you think? Would city life, with all its hustle and bustle, and things to do, suit your fancy? Or, would you rather live off the land where the pace of life follows the seasons, and you are busy with the duties of farm life?

¡VIVA LOS MEXICANOS!

Manuel Alvarez Bravo

Growing up in a large family that taught him to appreciate art, Manuel Bravo discovered his own special way of expressing his imagination and love for Mexico's people and places — through photography! The 1920s and 1930s were an exciting time in Mexico, when all kinds of artists were finding new ways of celebrating Mexico's traditional culture. Bravo tried to capture the spirit of Mexico in his photography that looked at ordinary people and objects in new ways. Perhaps you can take some photographs. What everyday objects can you photograph that would say what's important to you?

¿Hablas español?

Many Mexicans know some English — mostly learned by watching American TV shows and movies — but the language most commonly spoken is Spanish.

You probably already know some Spanish words such as tortilla *and* salsa. *Here are some other words and phrases you can sprinkle in your everyday speech or use to converse with a Spanish-speaking friend.*

Greetings
Hello: *Hola* (OH-lah)
How are you?: *¿Cómo estás?* (COH-moh eh-STAHS)
Good morning: *Buenos días* (BWAY-nohs DEE-ahs)
Good afternoon: *Buenas tardes* (BWAY-nahs TAR-dehs)
Good night: *Buenas noches* (BWAY-nahs NOH-chase)
Bye!: *¡Adiós!* (ah-dee-OHS)
See you later: *Hasta luego* (AHS-tah loo-EH-goh)

Favorite Beginning Phrases
Do you speak: *¿Hablas* (AH-blahs)...
  Spanish? *español?* (es-pahn-YOHL)
  English? *inglés?* (ing-LACE)
  French? *francés?* (fran-SEHS)
My name is: *Me llamo...* (may YAH-moh)
What is your name?: *¿Cómo te llamas?* (COH-moh tay YAH-mahs)
Play with us: *Juega con nosotros* (HWAY-gah cone noh-SOH-trohs)
Let's go: *Vámonos* (BAH-moh-nohs)

Key Words

Yes: *Sí* (see)
No: *No* (noh)
Please: *Por favor* (por fah-VOHR)
Thank you: *Gracias* (GRAH-see-ahs)
Friend: *Amigo* (male) (ah-MEE-goh);
 amiga (female) (ah-MEE-gah)
Good: *Bueno* (BWAY-noh)
Very good: *Muy bueno*
 (mooey BWAY-noh)
Cool!: *¡Padre!* (PAH-dray)

Colors

Red: *rojo* (ROH-hoh)
Orange: *anarajado* (ah-nar-an-HAH-tho)
Yellow: *amarillo* (ah-mah-REE-yoh)
Green: *verde* (BEAR-day)
Blue: *azul* (ah-SOOL)
Pink: *rosa* (ROH-sah)
Brown: *morado* (more-AH-tho)
White: *blanco* (BLAHN-coh)
Black: *negro* (NAY-groh)
Gray: *gris* (greese)

Let's Eat

I'm hungry: *Tengo hambre*
 (TANG-goh AHM-bray)
I want: *Yo quiero* (yo key-AIR-oh)...
Do you want: *¿Quieres* (key-AIR-race)
...milk: *leche* (LAY-cheh)
...juice: *jugo* (WHO-goh)
...bread: *pan* (pahn)
...beans: *frijoles* (free-HOH-lace)
...meat: *carne* (CAR-nay)
...cookies: *galletas* (guy-YET-ahs)
...ice cream: *helado* (eh-LAH-thoh)
...salsa: *salsa* (SAHL-sah)
...tortilla: *tortilla* (tor-TEE-ah)

Make a Sentence

I have: *Tengo* (TANG-goh)...
...a home: *una casa* (OO-nah CAH-sah)
...a car: *un coche* (oon COH-cheh)
...a dog: *un perro* (oon PAIR-roh)
...a cat: *un gato* (oon GAH-toh)
...a goldfish: *una carpa de oro*
 (OO-nah CAR-pah day OR-oh)

Un Perro

About Me

I like: *Me gusta* (may GOOSE-tah)...
Do you like: *¿Te gusta* (tay GOOSE-tah)
...to play: *jugar* (who-GAHR)
...to run: *correr* (core-RARE)
...to eat: *comer* (coh-MARE)
...to walk: *andar* (ahn-DAHR)
...to draw: *dibujar* (dee-boo-HAHR)
...to sing: *cantar* (cahn-TAHR)

Family Ties

I love you: *Te amo* (tay AH-moh)...
...Mom: *mamá* (mah-MAH)
...Dad: *papá* (pah-PAH)
...brother: *hermano* (air-MAH-noh)
...sister: *hermana* (air-MAH-nah)
...grandmother: *abuela* (ah-BWAY-lah)
...grandfather: *abuelo* (ah-BWAY-loh)

Un Gato

Feelings

I am: *Yo soy* (yo soy)...
You are: *Tu eres* (too AIR-ehs)...
Are you: *¿Eres* (AIR-ehs)...
...happy: *feliz* (fay-LEASE)
...sad: *triste* (TREESE-tay)
...funny: *chistoso* (male) (chees-TOH-so);
 chistosa (female) (chees-TOH-sah)
...nice: *simpático* (male) (sim-PAH-tee-coh);
 simpática (female) (sim-PAH-tee-cah)

For numbers 0 through 10 in Spanish, see page 41.

Don't forget to mix and match. With just these few Spanish words and phrases, you can actually carry on a conversation. To celebrate your new language, serve a Mexican dinner (page 27) and wear Mexican traditional clothes (page 50). ¡Muy bueno!

Play *Los Listones* (The Ribbons)

For this game, you need a group of your friends — and the Spanish words for colors (page 11).

One of the players is the Buyer, another the Seller, and the remaining players are Ribbons. The Buyer leaves the room; while she's gone, the Seller gives each of the Ribbons a color name. The Buyer enters and pretends to knock on a door.

"Rap, rap," says the Buyer.
"Who is it?" answers the Seller.
"Old (Buyer's name)," the Buyer replies.
"What do you want?" demands the Seller.
"To buy a ribbon," the Buyer replies.
"What color?" asks the Seller.

The Buyer then names a color (in Spanish, of course!). If it's a color of one of the Ribbons, that Ribbon joins the Buyer. Each time the Buyer guesses wrong, the Seller gets a Ribbon. The Buyer gets as many guesses as there are ribbon players. The winner ends up with the most Ribbons.

Other Tongues

Besides Spanish, over 50 Indian, or native, languages are spoken throughout Mexico. In fact, lots of Mexicans who speak these ancient languages are bilingual. That means they speak two languages — their native one and usually, Spanish.

Many North American children also speak two languages. In the Canadian province of Quebec, for example, both French and English are spoken. Many kids speak one language at home and with friends, and another at school.

Feasts and Fasts

Have you ever noticed how many religious traditions begin or end with a feast — or include a period of fasting?

The Mexicans feast as part of celebrating baptisms, birthdays, and the Day of the Dead.

Ask your friends of different religious and cultural backgrounds about their traditional feasts and fasts.

WELCOME, LITTLE STRANGER!

In Mexico, the most important events in a person's life — birth, marriage, and death — are marked by religious ceremonies. Many are Catholic traditions, but many Mexicans also observe much older customs deeply rooted in their cultural past.

Babies are welcomed into the world in special ways. The Maya (MY-ah), native peoples living in the southern states of Yucatán, Chiapas, Quintana Roo, and Campeche (see map, page 6), give their newborns gifts that represent what each child will need in later life. A baby girl might be given a stone used for grinding corn and a small piece of a loom, while baby boys may receive farming tools.

The Huichol (WEE-chohl) bestow their newborns with a special good-luck charm, known as an *Ojo de Dios* (OH-ho day dee-OHS), or God's Eye. Traditionally, just the "eye," or center, is made when the child is born. Then, on each birthday up to age 5, a section of yarn in a different color is added — a beautiful reminder of each year's celebration!

Mixtec art from Codex Nuttall

Make an *Ojo de Dios*

If you know a newborn child, perhaps you would like to mark the occasion of his or her birth by making an Ojo. You don't have to wait each year to add new sections of yarn to your Ojo, of course. Choose shades that match your favorite colors or that have special meaning to you.

YOU WILL NEED:
- 2 straight sticks
- Yarn, in a variety of colors

1. Cross the sticks in the middle and lash them together by wrapping yarn around them, first one way and then the other, until the yarn forms a rounded hump. This is the "eye."

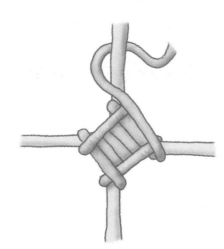

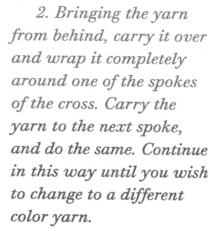

2. Bringing the yarn from behind, carry it over and wrap it completely around one of the spokes of the cross. Carry the yarn to the next spoke, and do the same. Continue in this way until you wish to change to a different color yarn.

To change color, simply tie on a new length of yarn near a spoke, so that the knot is hidden at the back.

3. Finish the Ojo with a knot near a spoke. Tie a hanging loop from the back.

ON THE DAY YOU WERE BORN

Birthdays in Mexico are big fun. The day often begins with the traditional birthday song *Las mañanitas*. Some families even hire a *mariachi* band to play it outside the birthday child's bedroom window!

Later in the day, there will probably be a party, much like birthday parties everywhere – excited children busily eating favorite foods and playing games like *Los listones* (page 12).

Children who live in Mexico's capital, Mexico City, sometimes have their parties in one of the city's large parks. Picnic foods are packed up, along with a *piñata* (page 17), ready to hang from a rope strung between two trees. Strolling musicians or mimes are sometimes hired to entertain everyone, too!

"The 'Typical' Band" by José Posada

THE SOUND OF MUSIC

If there's one sound that is Mexico, it's mariachi music! The distinctive music played by these strolling bands can be heard everywhere.

For a small fee, mariachi bands will happily serenade a loved one with a personal request. How about a rousing rendition of Las mañanitas? Maybe you would prefer a lament, or sad song, so typical of this kind of music.

If the music doesn't catch your ear, the fancy costumes will certainly catch your eye. Mariachis wear fancy outfits with short jackets and close-fitting trousers, usually studded with shiny decorations. And don't forget the hat! The musicians wear huge *sombreros*, often covered with sequins and colorful embroidery.

Compose a Lament

Compose your own lament or love song in the style of mariachi music. Most mariachi songs are written in rhyming verse — not surprising, considering that so many Spanish words end in "o," "a," and other repeated sounds.

Pair your words with an authentic mariachi melody (listen to Linda Ronstadt's Canciones de mi padre, *or one of Arhoolie Productions' many recordings of mariachi music for some typical tunes), or sing your words to a melody of your choice. Here's a verse from one song to get you thinking:*

> **Dear little one of my life,**
> **joy amidst my sorrows,**
> **I ask you not to forget me,**
> **for the rest of our tomorrows.**
> **I ask you not to forget me,**
> **wherever you might be.**

¡VIVA LOS MEXICANOS!

Carlos Chávez

Carlos Chávez, one of Mexico's most famous composers, believed it was important for Mexicans to create their own works of art, including music, for the whole world to see and hear. He became part of what is often called the "Mexican Renaissance," celebrating the past but adding the new.

Chávez thought about the art of the Aztec and Maya Indians, writing new music that expressed the spirit of those ancient peoples. Listen to some of Carlos Chávez's music: What images and feelings does it bring into your imagination? Can you feel the spirit of the ancient Mexicans?

Happy Birthdays to You!

How would you like to have two birthdays each year? Lots of Mexican children do! How's that, you say? Many children have a party to mark the date they were born, and also on the day of the saint for whom they are named. For instance, if you were born on June 3 and were named for St. Francis (who is honored by the Catholic church on October 4), then you'd celebrate your birthday on both of those days. So, Happy Birthdays to you!

Make a *Piñata*

Make your next birthday party a smash hit — with a homemade piñata, of course! (Make it a few days in advance, as the papier-mâché needs to dry.)

Make the flower shown here, or create your own design, such as an animal face or star. Mexican children often choose piñatas in the shapes of favorite cartoon characters.

YOU WILL NEED:

* Large, round balloon
* Newspaper
* Paste, made from equal amounts of flour and water
* Twine
* Paint and paintbrush
* Tissue paper
* Glue
* Rope

1. *Blow up the balloon and tie it. Tear some newspaper into short strips. Paste a layer of strips onto the balloon, overlapping them slightly.*

2. *Make a harness for the piñata by taping twine to the balloon as shown. Cover the balloon with three more layers of newspaper strips. Hang the balloon to dry in a warm place. This may take several days.*

CONTINUED

3. To make a flower, paint the balloon bright yellow dotted with orange dots; let dry. Cut large petals from tissue paper, and glue them all around the piñata.

4. Cut a trap door in the back of the piñata; carefully pop the balloon and remove it. Fill the piñata with goodies; then, close the trap door. Tie the harness to a rope, and you're ready to hang it!

Note: Throw out popped balloon. It is very dangerous to small children who can choke on it.

THE HIT OF THE PARTY!

Ask a grown-up to hang your piñata from a hook or tree branch. Take turns swinging at the piñata to break it. Give the blindfolded swinger a bat or large stick, twirl three times; then, let go! To make the piñata more difficult to hit, slowly raise and lower the rope holding it up.

Chant the chorus to this song Mexican children sing while swinging at piñatas.

Dale, dale, dale,
(DAH-lay, DAH-lay, DAH-lay)
No pierdas el tino,
(no pee-AIR-dahs el TEE-noh)
Que de la distancia
(kay day lah dees-TAHN-see-ah)
Se pierde el camino.
(say pee-AIR-day el cah-MEE-noh)

What do the words mean? Loosely translated:

**Hit it, hit it, hit it,
If you don't hit it,
you'll lose your way.**

HAPPY FAMILIES, HAPPY TIMES

Who are the most important people in your life? If you said the members of your family — your parents, your brothers and sisters, as well as your grandparents, aunts, uncles, and cousins — then you can easily understand why Mexicans value their family ties so much.

The ties Mexicans have with others in their community are also important and are further strengthened whenever Mexicans meet one another at the *mercado*, or market, gather in parks and plazas, or celebrate *fiestas*. Happy families coming together mean happy times!

THE FAMILY CIRCLE

Imagine living with your brothers, sisters, parents, and grandparents (and perhaps even an aunt, uncle, and a few cousins) — all under the same roof! Sounds pretty cozy, right? Believe it or not, it's not all that uncommon for many Mexican families. The best part of this arrangement is that family members take care of each other. Your grandparents can baby-sit while your parents are at work; all the adults can share in looking after your grandparents as they grow older.

If you are from a Maya family in the very southern part of Mexico, your family might take this one step further. In addition to relatives, you might establish a special relationship with another family. Your parents and the parents from the other family call each other *compadres*, or "co-parents," helping one another just the way families do.

The More, the Merrier

What's it like to live in close quarters with lots of people? Find out for yourself by packing a small crowd into a single room in your home some rainy day. You may find it's not that easy sharing a small space with so many others. How much time goes by before you start getting on each other's nerves? What do you find most difficult to tolerate in close quarters — no privacy, no space, no place to call your own? What would be the "keys" to making a shared living space workable?

Think About It

Just Like Family

Nowadays, families often live thousands of miles apart. How do they cope? Many have close friends and neighbors who pitch in to help — they take turns baby-sitting, celebrate holidays together, and are available in the event of emergencies. Who do you and your family share special events with? Who offers comfort in the rougher times?

LET'S EAT!

For some Mexicans, the midday meal is the biggest. It is served between 1:00 and 4:00 in the afternoon. Lucky for you, you've been invited to join a Mexican family for lunch. So, what's on the menu?

Lunch often begins with soup. One favorite is a tomato-flavored broth called *sopa de fideos* (SO-pah day fee-DAY-ohs), so thick with noodles you need a fork to eat it! Any number of tortilla dishes might follow — from *tacos* to *enchiladas*. And don't forget the salsa! There isn't a table in the country that doesn't have a bowl of salsa on it, ready to spoon on anything and everything!

If you have room for dessert, help yourself to some flan, one of Spain's most famous contributions to Mexican meals. Flan is egg custard with a caramel sauce. *¡Muy delicioso!*

Mix Up a Bowl of *Salsa*

This salsa is best eaten soon after it's made. (It tends to get watery, and the vegetables lose their crispness, if it stands too long.)

Chop ingredients into small pieces. Mix together, adding salt to taste. Let the flavors blend for 30 minutes. Spoon onto tacos or serve with tortilla chips. Makes 1 ½ cups (350 ml).

YOU WILL NEED:

* 1 tomato
* ½ medium onion
* 3 fresh green chiles (see note)
* 6 sprigs fresh cilantro, also known as coriander
* Salt

Note: For lots of bite, use *chiles serranos*, or any small, hot pepper. Choose a milder pepper for a salsa that is not quite as *picante* — or spicy!

Handle with Care

Some people with sensitive skin may be bothered when handling chile peppers. Wearing rubber gloves is a wise precaution to take. Also, wash your hands afterward, so that you don't sting your eyes.

SOME LIKE IT HOT

Some people think all Mexican food is spicy. Not true! Chile peppers — the main ingredient that adds bite to a dish — are used in many recipes, but only a few chiles are real tongue-burners. Most are more flavorful than fiery. (Usually, the smaller the chile, the hotter it is.)

Chiles show up in some surprising places in Mexican foods. Fruit stands sell fresh fruit squeezed with lime juice and sprinkled with — you guessed it! — dried, powdered chile. Chiles even show up in candies. One popular candy is nothing more than a tiny packet of granulated sugar mixed with salt, citric acid, and a powerful pinch of dried chiles!

MEXICO PAST

Behave Yourself!

The Aztec used chiles as a means of disciplining their children. Mischievous kids must have thought twice about being naughty if it meant suffering the sting of chiles!

FIRE! FIRE!

If you bite into some Mexican food that bites you right back, here's a trick for putting out the fire: Eat some bread — or other starchy food, such as a corn tortilla or potatoes — or drink some milk. While it's tempting to reach for a glass of water or soda, neither do much to soothe the burning sensation.

Make Your Own *Tortillas*

Have you ever eaten homemade tortillas? If not, you're in for a treat! Look for masa harina *(MAH-sah ah-REE-nah) in the international food section of your local supermarket or health-food store (cornmeal cannot be substituted). Be sure to get a grown-up's help when using the stove.*

YOU WILL NEED:
- 2 cups (250 g) masa harina
- 1⅓ (315 ml) cups water
- Waxed paper
- Griddle or fry pan

1. Heat the ungreased griddle on the stove over medium heat. Meanwhile, combine the masa harina and water in a bowl. Mix well.

2. Divide the dough into 10 even pieces, rolling each into a smooth ball. Press each ball into a flat circle, or flatten with a rolling pin. (Flatten between two sheets of waxed paper to avoid stickiness.)

3. Cook each tortilla on the griddle for one minute; then, turn over and cook for about 30 seconds, or until heated through. Keep the cooked tortillas warm in a basket lined with a cloth. Makes ten 6-inch (15-cm) tortillas.

Note: If the dough crumbles when you're patting it, add a tiny bit more water. If it sticks to the waxed paper, add a little more masa harina.

Grind Some Corn

How did the ancient Mexicans prepare the corn they ate? Probably the same way Mexicans in remote areas of the country still do today. The dried kernels were first boiled in a solution of water and lime (not the fruit, but a substance made from heated limestone). The kernels were then placed on a metate *(may-TAH-tay), or flat grinding stone, and ground into a moist dough with a* mano *(MAH-noh), or hand-held stone.*

Try your hand at grinding some corn for fun. Soak a handful of popping corn in water overnight. Find a flat stone to use as a metate, and a smaller one for the mano. Then flex your muscles ... and grind!

metate

mano

The Good Old Days!

THEN & NOW Most people agree that machine-made tortillas just don't taste as good as homemade ones. Have you ever heard your grandparents — or even your parents — complain about how things were better back when they were growing up? Just what is it about the "good old days" that people seem to long for? Were the hot dogs at the ball park really that good — or is it something else?

¡GRACIAS, MÉXICO!

Try to imagine Italian food without tomatoes, Indian curries and Thai dishes without the bite of chiles, Thanksgiving without turkey, and a world without chocolate. It's hard, isn't it? Did you know that these, and many other of the world's most beloved and delicious foods, got their start in Mexico?

Some of these — such as corn, beans, and squash — traveled from Mexico thousands of years ago and were adopted by North America's native peoples. Others were exported only in the last 450 years or so when the Spaniards took samples back to Europe. From there, many of these foods made their way to other corners of the globe.

So, the next time you bite into a buttery ear of corn, pour tomato catsup on your French fries, or lick a vanilla (yes, vanilla, too!) ice-cream cone, take a moment to say, *"¡Gracias, México!"*

SUNDAY IN THE CITY

Mexico City is a bustling, noisy city. But the city turns into a different place altogether on weekends. Sundays, especially, are a leisurely time, a day when whole families go to the park. The city's largest park, Bosque de Chapultepec, is a favorite destination, with plenty of quiet tree-filled hideaways, as well as several wonderful museums and a zoo.

EL PASEO

On warm evenings, local parks belong to the young at heart. Groups of teen-aged girls stroll around the park, every so often passing groups of teen-aged boys parading in the opposite direction. Their parents are probably sitting on nearby park benches, or strolling several paces behind. They are keeping a watchful eye on their youngsters, happy that this age-old tradition, called *el paseo* (el pah-SAY-oh), is still alive. Many remember meeting their wives or husbands in just this way.

Think About It

Hanging Out

El paseo is not so different than "hanging out" American- and Canadian-style. In fact, in most Western cultures, guys and gals like to hang out somewhere around town. Problem is, many communities no longer have a place where older kids are welcome.

Is there a safe place to gather with friends where you live?

A FEAST FOR THE SENSES!

It's market day! The air is filled with delicious aromas, colorful sights, and the sounds of merchants and shoppers haggling over prices. It's truly a feast for all the senses.

You wander into the section where fruits and vegetables are sold. All are beautifully displayed: onions peeled of their papery skins and arranged in glistening mounds; tropical fruits like guavas and papayas all piled here and there; and bananas in every size, shape, and color imaginable. Fresh flowers in a rainbow of colors are bunched in tall containers. What shall you buy?

In another part of the mercado, or market, vendors sell meat, poultry, and fish. Is all this food making you a little hungry? You're in luck. There are plenty of food stands selling all sorts of tasty tidbits. Care for some freshly squeezed fruit juice? How about a taco?

Outside the market, seated on the ground,

you see women dressed in embroidered clothing, their heads covered by folded cloths. They come from nearby villages that still observe traditional ways. Some have hand-woven blankets and clothing for sale. Others sit behind mounds of dried herbs, each labeled with the condition or illness the plant is supposed to help. Do you know a young child suffering from dry nostrils? Powdered apricot kernels placed in them just might solve the problem!

Our Daily Bread

In many parts of Mexico, home refrigerators are uncommon, so items that spoil easily, such as milk and meat, are purchased each day. Even people with refrigerators and freezers often buy fresh foods daily.

Would daily shopping work for your family? See for yourself by trying it for a few days. Will it be easy to adjust to this new routine? Does buying food daily affect what you buy and eat in unexpected ways. Do you buy more "extras" every day? Does it cost more overall to shop daily? Take more time? Do you eat more junk food or less?

PARTY TIME!

Mexicans love to party! In fact, Mexico just might be the party country of the world. Most villages and city neighborhoods honor patron saints, but they also whoop it up for local heroes, at harvesttime, or when favorite flowers are in full bloom. Some celebrations trace their origins to Mexico's ancient native cultures, while others were introduced by the Spaniards.

CELEBRATE WITH A MEXICAN *FIESTA*

You can honor Mexican culture and people with a party anytime!

To get everyone in a fiesta mood, decorate your party space with red, green, and white — the colors of Mexico's flag — crepe paper streamers, or cut and hang lots of papel picado *banners (page 28). Ask a local travel agent for Mexican travel posters. Hang these and traditional crafts, such as an Ojo de Dios (page 14) or colorful weavings (page 51), on the walls.*

Don't forget to plan a menu of Mexican foods. You may already have some favorite recipes for tacos or burritos. Use your own homemade

tortillas (page 23) and salsa (page 21) to make these dishes extra special.

Make a piñata (page 17) to include in your festivities.

Don some festive clothing, put on some traditional or popular Mexican music, and greet everyone in Spanish (page 10). ¡Muy bueno!

Snip *Papel Picado* Banners

During festive occasions, Mexico is literally draped with colorful banners made from cut tissue paper. Known as papel picado (pah-PELL pee-CAH-thoh), or pierced paper, these colorful decorations have been made in Mexico since tissue paper was imported from Asia over 400 years ago. Some banners are purely decorative, while others include scenes, even words, fitting to the particular occasion. Papel picado banners turn any space, indoors or out, into a fiesta waiting to happen.

YOU WILL NEED:

- Tissue paper in assorted colors
- Scissors
- Glue
- String

1. To make one banner, cut a rectangle from tissue paper. Fold down a 1-inch (2.5-cm) hanging flap along the length of the paper. Now, fold the paper in half crosswise so that the flap is on the outside. Fold the paper in half two more times, just up to the flap, as shown.

fold once more

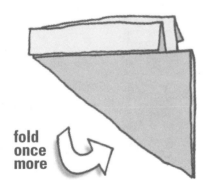

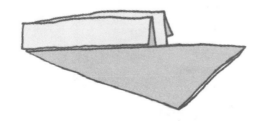

2. Shape the outer edge with scissors; then, snip designs along the folded edge. Unfold the paper once and snip at the bottom folded edge. Carefully open the paper, leaving the flap folded down.

3. *Fold and snip as many banners as you need to span the space you're decorating. To hang the banners, cut a piece of string slightly longer than your space. Open the hanging flap of each banner and place over the string; glue the flap down. Once all the banners are glued on, pin or tape the string in place.*

Tiny Flags

Make tiny papel picado banners and glue them onto toothpicks to make decorations you can stick into sandwiches, a cake, cupcakes, or fruit pieces. (Use for your topo map, too. See page 31.)

The First Mexicans

During the Ice Age – a period that ended about 10,000 years ago – a land bridge linked the continents of Asia and North America. The first people to set foot in Mexico actually came from northeast Asia, crossing into North America over this land bridge, where the Bering Strait is located today. Quite a journey! No one knows for sure when these first small groups of people traveled over this stretch of land, but it surely took many, many generations before people finally reached and settled in what is modern-day Mexico.

The terrain, or type of land, these first inhabitants discovered has changed little since then. Mexico still has it all – sandy beaches, lush rainforests, scrubby deserts, snow-capped peaks – even volcanoes!

THE LAY OF THE LAND

If you were to stand on either Mexico's west or east coast, you could wiggle your toes in the salty water. That's because the land there is at sea level (see map, page 31).

But head inland, and you'd better be prepared for a steady, uphill climb. Running down along either side of the country are two mountain chains — like the two long braids of an Indian woman, as they have been described.

The southern region is also mountainous. Some of the tallest peaks are snow-covered all year long!

Plant life varies a lot, too. Parts of northern Mexico are very dry, so not much grows there except grasses and cactus. The southern part of the country is just the opposite. That's where the most rain falls each year and the country's tropical rainforest is located.

DID YOU KNOW?

Mexico's climate is tropical, which means there are only two seasons — a dry season and a rainy one. Plants grow best during the rainy season, which lasts from about the end of November to the end of May.

Make a "Topo" Map

A topographical map shows land three-dimensionally with its mountains, plateaus, and river beds. You can see, just by looking at it, why people were isolated, what they probably ate, if they traded, and what problems they faced. The lay of the land has a big story to tell.

YOU WILL NEED:

⚜ **Scrap paper**
⚜ **Blender**
⚜ **White glue**
⚜ **Masonite or thin, stable board**
⚜ **Tempera paint and paintbrush**

MEXICO

GULF OF MEXICO

Plateaus
Mountains
Rain forests
Rivers and lakes

PACIFIC OCEAN

CONTINUED

1. *Tear paper into small pieces; soak in water for about an hour. With a grown-up's help, blend small amounts of the soggy paper — in plenty of extra water — to make pulp. After each batch, squeeze the moisture out and place pulp in a bowl. When you have about two cups of pulp, mix in enough white glue to make a stiff modeling material.*

2. *Draw a large outline of Mexico on the board. Use the pulp to fill in the outline, building it up for the mountain chains and for the high plateaus between them. Place the model in a warm spot and let dry (this may take several days).*

3. *Paint the map, perhaps with the mountains brown, plateaus green, oceans blue, and any other details. Add a color key.*

ON THE MOVE

The first Mexicans were nomads, or people who moved about in a large, "home" territory of land, in search of food. The ancients had cutting tools with the sharpest cutting edges known to humans, made with blades of obsidian, a dark, volcanic glass. They probably ate lots of smaller animals like rabbits and lizards, with an occasional wolf and deer — even a mammoth! — thrown in. No doubt, they also caught fish to eat. But, mostly, these early inhabitants munched on plants. They roamed from spot to spot, stopping wherever there were water and good eating, then moving on when the food ran out or the streams dried up.

Where did they sleep? They probably sought shelter in caves, but they also built shelters. On clear nights, they may have slept in the open air under the stars. This big, wide world with its open spaces was also where babies were born, and where the sick and the old people died. What an incredible experience living must have been for these first wandering peoples!

DID YOU KNOW?

Many of us imagine that nomads wandered from place to place, which is only partially true. Yes, they did wander, very likely in search of new plant life to eat. But, they didn't wander to completely new places; instead, they wandered in a "home" territory, eventually returning to where they had been before.

Go FIGURE

A generation is a group of people all about the same age. You and your friends of about the same age are one generation. Your parents and their friends are another generation. Your grandparents belong to yet another generation.

A generation is about 25 years, or the average time needed for children to have children of their own.

If a group of people left Asia 20,000 years ago, and their descendants arrived in Mexico, say, 12,000 years ago, how many generations did it take before there were people living in the area now known as Mexico? (To get started, subtract 12,000 from 20,000. Keep the 25 years per generation in mind as you proceed.) Compare your answer with the one at the bottom of the page.

Answer: 20,000–12,000 = 8,000 years journey, 8,000 ÷ 25 = 320 generations!

SETTLING DOWN

Eventually, Mexico's early foragers began to also grow some of the plants they ate, leading to their staying in one spot. Not surprisingly, they chose places to live where the soil was fertile and where water was plentiful, like in central Mexico and along the Pacific Coast.

Which plants did the early Mexicans first grow? Most likely beans and squash, then maize, or corn, and tomatoes, chile peppers, and avocados.

Maya maize god

AMAZING MAIZE

Archaeologists, people who study history from the remains of ancient places, agree that corn was the crop that made even the early settlements of Mexico possible. Kernels of corn over 9,000 years old have been found in caves in the south central part of the country!

Ancient corn was very different from today's grain. The ear was teeny tiny, barely an inch (2.5 cm) long. The tassels were only found at the very top of the ear. Over thousands of years, corn grew in size – both the plant itself (which is a type of grass) and the ears. Today, many types of corn are grown in Mexico, from plants that bear ears with soft kernels eaten right off the cob to corn with hard kernels that are perfect for popping or grinding.

MEXICO TODAY

Mexico's topography continues to influence the lives of its people. The mountainous regions of the north are rugged, and the people who make their homes there live very simply, largely isolated from the rest of Mexico. It's just the opposite on Mexico's two coasts. Many coastal towns are bustling, modern places: Several serve as shipping ports, while others are popular vacation spots for tourists.

The Rest of the Story

Archaeologists remind us that conditions for preserving ancient foods in Mexico were right only in certain places. So, while the oldest remains of corn were found in central Mexico, this doesn't mean it wasn't raised earlier somewhere else.

Our understanding of ancient history usually depends on what artifacts have been preserved. But what happens when artifacts only tell half the story?

enlarged view of early corn

THE OLMEC CIVILIZATION

Very little is known of the Olmec, the first great civilization in Mexico, other than that their civilization thrived along the warm and wet Gulf Coast from around 1200 to 400 B.C.

We don't know how many people lived in the Olmec settlements, or how their once-thriving centers came to an end. Sadly, many communities appear to have been destroyed intentionally, with monuments smashed, and the rubble buried in long trenches. Whether this was done by invading peoples, or whether there was unrest within the communities themselves, nobody knows for sure. Because the Olmec left little more than some examples of their art behind, this may always be a mystery.

Kunz axe made of jade

Think About It

Do you think people will view world events of the late 20th century differently in 100 years? How about in 500 years?

Think About It

How do topography and climate affect you and your lifestyle?

Mark Your Topo Map

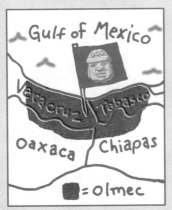

Mark the borders of the Olmec civilization by making one-color flags out of toothpicks and construction paper (see page 29). Start a map flag key, noting the color that equals Olmec. Continue for each civilization you meet on your journey through Mexico. See the time line on page 53, too.

Naming Names

No one knows what the Olmec called themselves. They were named nearly three thousand years later after a people who lived in the same region then.

Olmec is a Náhuatl word meaning "Rubber People." Rubber has long been harvested from trees in the region and used to waterproof baskets. Even though the Olmec probably didn't call themselves Rubber People, researchers of this ancient civilization believe the name describes what was probably an important part of their culture.

ART FOR ART'S SAKE

The Olmec were the first Mexicans to create art for its own sake — to be admired and appreciated, and not just as decoration on useful objects, such as pottery.

Most of the Olmec art that has survived is made from carved stone. Some of the smaller pieces, such as figurines, beads, and ceremonial axes, are made from the gemstone jade. Larger works were made from volcanic rock, which is all the more fascinating when you realize this type of rock is not found at the Olmec sites; it had to be brought down from mountains as far as 60 miles (96 km) away!

Certainly the most amazing examples of Olmec art are huge free-standing heads carved from volcanic rock. Some of these stand over 9 feet (3 m) high and weigh as much as 40 tons (36,364 kg)! These giant heads are believed to be portraits of Olmec rulers.

Sticks, Stones, and Names

Sometimes when people don't know how to refer to others, they call them a name that makes sense to them, such as the "Rubber People." But sometimes, names — especially nicknames — can be hurtful. Has anyone ever hurt your feelings by referring to you in a way that felt insulting? One easy way around this problem is to say, "I like to be called…. What do you like to be called?"

Carve an Olmec-Style Head

The Olmec stone heads are shown wearing close-fitting helmets carved with distinctive designs. Similar helmets were worn when playing a sacred ball game (page 47).

Carve your own Olmec-style head. (Make two and you'll have a pair of bookends.) Here's one way to do it:

(page 47)

YOU WILL NEED:
- Plastic bucket
- Plaster of Paris
- Coffee grounds
- Bottom half of a half-gallon (2 L) milk carton
- Carving tools, such as chisel, small hack saw, and nails

DID YOU KNOW?

The Olmec made all their stone carvings without using metal tools. How could they cut such a hard material? They wore away at the stone by rubbing it with damp sand. To cut larger pieces of stone into slabs, they ground the sand into the stone with a piece of rope pulled back and forth. What tool does this back-and-forth action remind you of?

1. *In a plastic bucket, mix up some plaster of Paris according to package instructions. Add a handful of coffee grounds to color the mixture and give it a stone-like texture. Pour the plaster into the milk carton half; set aside to harden.*

2. *Remove the carton; then, carve the plaster block to resemble an Olmec head. With grown-up help, use the tools to smooth the sharp corners of the block and to carve the features and helmet decorations.*

The Ancient World of the Maya

Long before Europeans were crowning their kings, knighting their knights, and building cathedrals during the Middle Ages (900 B.C. – A.D. 1500), a group of people across the Atlantic Ocean had already studied the sun's rotation, mapped the stars, mastered math, and developed a communication system using pictures, called hieroglyphs. They also invented the calendar we rely on to navigate us through the year. Who were these people so ahead of their time? Most anthropologists say they were descendants of the ancient Olmec, a people known as the Maya (MY-uh).

Without the help of horses, mules, metal tools, or the wheel, this mysterious civilization that was at its peak from about A.D. 250 until A.D. 900 (about 15 centuries ago) created massive pyramids, towering sacrificial temples, and enormous stone cities many times larger than those in Europe at that time.

LINK TO THE PAST

Many aspects of Olmec culture were also a part of Maya life. How did the two civilizations come to have so many similarities? Some anthropologists (people who study civilizations) believe the Maya were actually descended from the ancient Olmec. Others think the early Maya learned from the Olmec when trading with them. Or, perhaps there was a battle and the Maya learned from Olmec prisoners or slaves. Whatever happened, the ancient Maya adopted and refined many Olmec customs and practices. And, so we see the beginning of an intertwining of cultures, Olmec and Maya, as well as the forward movement of the past into a new present.

The Maya dwelled in what are now the southern Mexican states of Chiapas and Yucatán, and neighboring Central American countries Guatemala and Belize.

Put one-colored marker flags on your topo map and key, defining the Maya area.

Maya waterside village, Chichén Itzá, Yucatán

ALPHABET SOUP

Have you ever seen dates of events written 400 B.C. or A.D. 1500? These letters are a way of marking the modern Western calendar, showing the dates from zero forward as the time from the birth of Christ forward. You may also see the dates noted this way: B.C.E., means Before the Common Era, (same as B.C.) and C.E., means Common Era (same as A.D.).

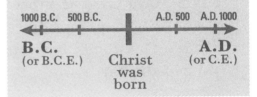

| 1000 B.C. | 500 B.C. | | A.D. 500 | A.D. 1000 |

B.C.
(or B.C.E.)

Christ
was
born

A.D.
(or C.E.)

More Alike than Different

The ancient Maya have been called the "Greeks of the Americas," because of their accomplishments in science. They've also been compared to the Romans (because of the extensive road systems they built), the Egyptians (because of their pyramids), and the Phoenicians (because of their ocean-going travels on trading missions). Maybe we should recognize them for their own accomplishments!

MASTERS OF THE UNIVERSE

The ancient Maya developed their ideas about time by carefully watching the sky. By observing daily, monthly, and yearly changes in the heavens, they learned the cycles of day and night, plus those of the moon, sun, stars, and several of the planets. They were even able to accurately predict when solar eclipses would occur.

The Maya created two calendars — one 365 days long (just like the calendar we use today, based on the year-long journey of the earth around the sun), and one 260 days long.

The Sky's the Limit

While scanning the heavens, the Maya were also hoping to get signals from the gods. What kind of signals? Messages ranging from the best time to plant crops to warnings about upcoming natural disasters or even when to wage war.

It's easy to see for yourself just what the Maya were observing. Each night after dark, go outside and look up into the sky. Notice the way the shape of the moon changes.

Is it always in the same place? Mark the moon's phases on a calendar every night for an entire month. Draw what you see, noting the direction the open part of the crescent faces both before the moon is full, and afterwards. Look for other clues, too. Does a clear sky bring certain weather conditions? What about a starless night? While you're sky-watching, ask yourself what messages the Maya might have gotten from the sky.

WHAT IS IT?

Keeping in mind their interest in the sky, can you solve the following Maya riddle?

What is it?
A blue bowl filled with popcorn.

Give up? Check below for the answer.

Answer: *The night sky, dotted with stars.*

Pick a Number

The Maya kept track of time with numbers, using special symbols called glyphs, adopted from earlier peoples.

The ancient number system, which is based on increments of 20, is very different from the one we use today that's based on the number 10. The figures for 0 through 19, however, are easy to understand. They are written using only three symbols:

a shell = 0   a dot = 1   a bar = 5

Here's what the numbers zero through 19 looked like:

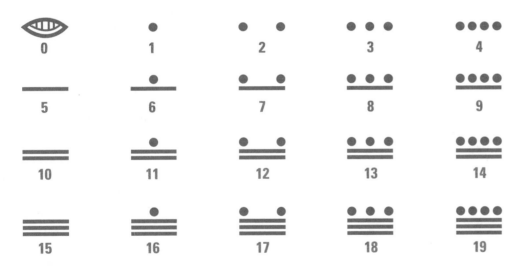

Try using these numbers to do some simple arithmetic. Can you solve the following problems? Write your answers in Maya glyphs, of course! Check your results with the answers below.

A.

B.

C.

D.

DID YOU KNOW?

Some historians think the ancient Mexicans were the very first to understand the concept of zero. Some think the shell that represents the Maya zero symbolized an empty oyster shell. During festivities, oysters on the half shell were eaten by party-goers, and empty shells meant no oysters — or zero oysters. What do you think?

COUNTING TO TEN

Now that you know how to count to 10 the ancient Maya way, here's how to say the first ten numbers in modern Spanish.

0: cero (SAIR-oh)
1: uno (OO-noh)
2: dos (dohs)
3: tres (trace)
4: cuatro (KWAH-troh)
5: cinco (SINK-oh)
6: seis (sayss)
7: siete (see-EH-tay)
8: ocho (OH-choh)
9: nueve (NWAY-vay)
10: diez (dee-ESS)

So how much are three dots plus one bar in Spanish? How about one bar times a shell?

Answers: *Ocho; Cero*   Answers: A. 13, B. 15, C. 14, D. 12

THE STRUCTURE OF SOCIETY

For many years, historians believed the ancient Maya were quiet, peace-loving peasants whose lives were guided by their priests. Judging by their beautiful art and architecture, they seemed to enjoy both stability and prosperity. It looked as if Maya times were happy times.

The Maya way of life, however, wasn't as simple or peaceful as many first believed. From studying ancient ruins, art, and codices (books), it is believed that priests were only part of a small, upper-class group that controlled government, warfare, and religion. This ruling class demanded the commoners contribute a large share of the food they grew and goods they made to the rulers and to the gods. Maya cities were not just places of worship; they were places of power where the ruling classes enjoyed many luxuries, while most of those who served them lived in poverty, like slaves.

WITH PRIDE AND SHAME

It's important to look at all aspects of a culture to understand it. Many cultures that accomplished great things have also endured episodes that caused great shame. While the Maya were learning about the cosmos and creating awe-inspiring works of architecture, they also conquered other peoples and held them prisoner.

Think About It

Mexicans are proud of the ancient civilizations that once thrived in their country. At the same time, many Mexicans treat modern-day Indians — descendants of the people who created these once-great societies — as second-class citizens.

Native Americans and the Inuit in North America suffer a similar fate. Why do you think this happens? What might help to change these attitudes?

Maya warriors with slaves

MEXICO TODAY

Ancient Religion— Alive and Well

While most modern-day Maya attend church, praying to a Christian God and saints, many continue to pay tribute to their ancient gods. (In some communities, the sun and Jesus Christ are worshipped as one.) Village elders who still remember "the old ways" perform age-old rituals following the ancient Maya calendar. There are ceremonies to bring rain, cure illnesses, and bring good fortune.

Blood is still an important part of many rituals, too. When a Maya baby is born, for example, blood from its umbilical cord is dripped onto an ear of corn. The kernels are later planted in a special plot. When the corn is eventually harvested and eaten, it symbolizes the bond between the child and the family.

god of maize and life

god of death and disease

ALMIGHTY GODS

As it did for all ancient Mexicans, religion played a major role in daily Maya life. Gods were credited with moving the sun across the sky, bringing rain, as well as protecting everything from growing crops to women in childbirth.

The Maya offered the gods tributes — food, drink, even human blood. They believed that an important trade of human blood for rain was needed to insure the survival of both the gods and the Maya themselves. Men and women used stingray spines to draw blood from their own bodies. Others were sacrificed at the hands of priests. These brutal acts were considered essential at the time. It was actually an honor to sacrifice your life, if it meant maintaining order between the gods and humans.

TALL TALES

The ancient Maya shed their own blood in order to bring rain. Rain, of course, was necessary for growing corn, the all-important crop the Maya called "sunbeam of the gods." The following tale about the origins of corn brings smiles to the faces of Maya children to this day.

WHEN CORN WAS HIDDEN

The ancients used to say that one year the animals ran out of food. Fox noticed that while everyone else went hungry, the ants appeared well fed. He decided to see how this could be. Spying on them one day, Fox saw that the ants disappeared into an opening in a pile of rocks, then emerged carrying kernels of white corn. So that was it! Fox also noticed that the ants dropped some of the kernels. He picked them up and so had something to eat himself.

None of the other animals would have suspected anything had they not noticed that Fox's breath was sweeter than usual. Try as they might, they were unable to get the wily creature to tell them what he'd been eating or where it was hidden. So they decided to spy on Fox. They watched while the ants marched out of the opening in the rocks and they saw how Fox scurried to pick up the dropped kernels.

Of course, there were not enough dropped kernels for all the animals. There was no way to get to the kernels without breaking the rocks. The animals decided to ask three lightning bolts to help them. The first two bolts couldn't even make a dent in the stone, but the third had a better idea. He asked Woodpecker to tap on the rock with his beak to find where the rock was thinnest. Woodpecker was happy to help, but in his excitement forgot to move out of the way when the third bolt struck. (The lightning scorched the top of the bird's head, which is red to this day.)

The corn came pouring out, only it, too, was changed. The heat of the lightning bolt had turned some of the white kernels red. The smoke had turned some yellow, and some were burnt as black as night. And that's why Indian corn looks the way it does today.

In Your Own Words

Invent your own folktale to explain something about corn — perhaps how people learned to cook and grind it — or about other popular Mexican foods. What kind of story might you tell to explain how chiles got their spiciness, or how the avocado came to have such a large pit?

STEP BY STEP

When you think of pyramids, you probably think of Egypt, home of the ancient world's best-known pyramids. But did you know that the Mexicans — from the Olmec to the Maya, plus many others — were also pyramid-builders?

Mexican pyramids, known as step pyramids, are constructed like layer cakes, with the layers getting smaller as the pyramids rise. Most were actually built as platforms for temples that were placed at the very top.

Mexicans and visitors to Mexico today can explore these crumbling but still impressive structures. You can imagine just how awe-inspiring they must have been when they were in their glory!

Think About It

Pyramids tower above the other buildings found at Mexican archaeological sites. The ancient Mexicans thought of them as artificial mountains, placing the temples as near to the heavens as possible.

Can you think of other tall buildings that were built for similar reasons? How about churches and cathedrals, with their high ceilings and towering steeples? Or, the Parthenon, a temple built by the ancient Greeks, atop the highest hill in Athens?

BURY ME NOT

For a long time, it was believed that none of the pyramids in the Americas were used as tombs, as the ones in Egypt were. But now we know some did hold the remains and riches of people of noble birth, most usually kings.

The Temple of the Inscriptions in Palenque, in the southern state of Chiapas, is the site of one such burial chamber. Located deep in the base of a pyramid, the room held a huge carved stone sarcophagus (sar-CAHF-ah-gus), or casket, in which the skeleton of Pacal, one of Palenque's kings, was found. His body was surrounded by literally pounds of jade jewelry and accessories. He wore bracelets on both arms, rings on all his fingers, a breastplate made from nearly 200 highly polished jade pieces, plus a jade mosaic mask that was placed over his face.

Maya sarcophagus lid

Build a Maya Step Pyramid

Construct a tabletop step pyramid from Legos® or other small building blocks in your home, or make a larger version from cardboard blocks. If you live where it snows, make one outdoors using the wintry white stuff.

For something truly out of the ordinary, *make an edible pyramid! Whip up a batch or two of your favorite cake recipe; bake in rectangular pans. Cut three or four squares from the cooked cake, each slightly smaller than the previous piece. Assemble the pieces into a step pyramid; then, frost and decorate with Mexican-style designs.*

MEXICO PAST

Making Do

For all their achievements, the Maya did not have metal tools, because hard metals weren't available in local mines. Gold, silver, and copper were mined and made into decorative objects, but they're too soft to make into tools. All the stone carving done in Mexico, until the Spaniards' arrival in the early 1500s, was done using only stone tools.

GAME OF THE GODS

Near many Mexican pyramids are the ruins of "H"-shaped ball courts used to play a sacred ball game. Probably first played by the Olmec, the game was neither a sport nor an amusement, but instead a competition with religious meaning. It was hardly fun for the losers: Players of the losing team sometimes had their heads chopped off after a game!

From what we know, each team was made up of 10 players who wore

Maya ball court marker

thick, protective coverings on their hips, elbows, and heads. Using all parts of the body except the hands, they had to keep a hard rubber ball from hitting the ground. Artwork of the time shows the game in action — players lunging, even skidding on the ground — to keep the ball airborne. Because the stakes were so high, players must have played as fiercely as they could, making it a very dangerous game!

Play Ball!

A similar ball game, played just for fun, is still played during certain festivals in the states of Nayarit and Sinaloa on the west coast of Mexico. Known as Tlachtli *(TLAHCHT-lee), the game is played by teams on a flat field divided into sections.*

Invite a group of friends to play a version of this game. Mark off a rectangular area into two halves; divide each half midway with a line. Using a Hacky Sack or bean bag, have teams take turns moving the sack from the center line back toward their own midway mark without letting it hit the ground. Players may use any part

of their bodies but their hands. If the sack hits the ground, it's the other team's turn. Score five points for each time a team succeeds in crossing its own mid-line. The first team to score 25 is the winner.

MIRROR, MIRROR ON MY SOUL

Many examples of art, from lifelike pottery figurines to painted murals, have been uncovered at Maya sites, teaching us about ancient Maya society. We know a lot about the importance of priests and the majesty of noblemen. We know what people once wore, what they ate, even how they amused themselves.

Some Maya art shows men gazing into mirrors. Were they checking to see that their feathers were in place, or were they looking for something else?

In the land of the Maya, mirrors symbolized power and leadership. A great Maya lord was expected to be "the mirror of his people." Does this mean he was meant to look like them or act like them? What do you think?

MEXICO TODAY

Hit, Kick, and Wallop!

Today, several ball sports are enjoyed around Mexico. While most are imports from other countries, none would be possible were it not for Mexico's ancient invention of the rubber ball!

The most popular is soccer, which Mexicans call *fútbol* (FOOT-bowl). Jai alai (hi ah-LIE) is an indoor game played with a small rubber ball hurled from a curved basket. It made its way to Mexico with the Spanish.

The most recent fad in ball sports comes from the United States. American baseball — spelled *beisbol* in Spanish — has lately taken Mexico by storm.

Lessons from Art

Artwork from ancient times tells us about the people of the time — or does it? Often, portraits were made of important or wealthy people, shown dressed in their finest clothing and doing "important" things. We may learn little about the "common people," who were not considered important enough to be shown in art.

Visit an art museum or take a look at some popular works of art in art books at the library. What can you learn from the painting about clothing, furniture, food, buildings, relationships? Let the art speak to you and tell you its story.

EYE OF THE BEHOLDER

What did the ancient Maya see when they gazed into their mirrors?

The Maya were a handsome people with strong, shapely noses. But if you look closely at samples of their art, you can see that their heads were oddly shaped. The forehead sloped back at an angle, while the head itself came almost to a point.

The Maya weren't born looking like this, of course. This was something the ruling classes did to their children. Babies were strapped into cradle boards that had a front part that pushed down on a child's forehead. The skull bones of a newborn are quite soft, and in a few days' time a baby's head would take on the shape the Maya found so pleasing.

The ancient Maya also thought crossed eyes were desirable. They would hang a tiny bead from a lock of hair hanging between a child's eyes. As the child focused on the ball, the eyes would cross and stay that way.

Think About It

Throughout history, people have changed the way they look to conform to current ideas of beauty. Ask a grown-up what kids used to do to make themselves be "in style." What are some ways — large or small — that people you know try to change their appearances to make themselves attractive? If someone says, "He/she is a beautiful person," what do you think is meant?

WEARABLE ART

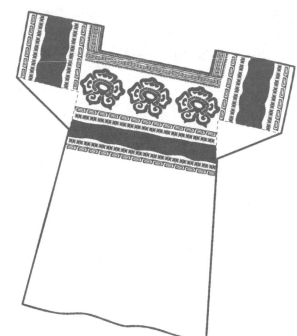

Some of the most beautiful clothing in Mexico today is made and worn by the Maya. In the highlands of Chiapas, woven and embroidered designs are so varied and distinctive that you can tell which village a person comes from just by looking at the clothes!

Traditional clothing is found mostly in smaller villages and worn most often by women. Most wear a top called a *huipile* (WEE-peel), a straight, usually sleeveless blouse, often decorated with embroidery. Under this is a long skirt, a tube-like length of fabric cinched in with a woven belt.

Stamp Out a Pattern

The designs on a huipile are more than just pretty. They are mystic symbols that connect the garment's maker and wearer with the gods. The weaver's position in the community — and the universe — is shown "in code," using both designs and color. Patterns are repeated, not for looks, but so that the gods will be sure to notice them.

Stamp your own Maya-style patterns on a T-shirt or tote bag. First, carve simple designs into potato halves (or draw onto a piece of Styrofoam). Stamp the designs on the fabric with waterproof paint. Experiment with zigzags, which represent the Maya lightning god, or toads, associated with rain. Play around with interlocking plant designs, or two-headed animals.

COLOR-CODED

The Maya associated certain colors with the four directions. East — where the sun rises — was the most important direction and was represented by *red. Black* symbolized west; *white,* north, and *yellow,* south. Like the Olmec before them, the Maya regarded *green* — the color of new corn and of water — as the color of life.

Weave a Popsicle-Loom Belt

Belts are popular throughout Mexico and are essential in the land of the Maya. Many beliefs are associated with belts, which are thought to protect the wearer from illnesses and give him or her strength to do the day's work.

Dress up an outfit with a colorful sash you weave yourself. Choose some of the traditional Maya colors, as described on page 50.

YOU WILL NEED:
- **Popsicle stick heddle loom (see box, page 52)**
- **Yarn**
- **Small piece of stiff cardboard**

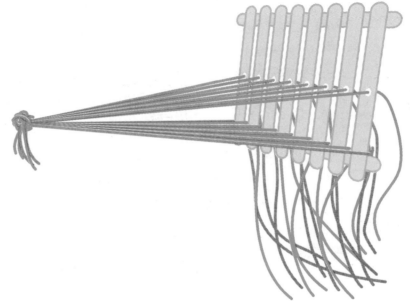

1. Cut 17 strands of yarn 6 feet (2 m) long. Arrange them in a striped pattern. Tie the strands together at one end; thread the loom by inserting a strand through each hole and on either side of each stick.

2. Pull the yarn evenly tight; knot the other end. Stretch the yarn between two objects, such as a doorknob and a chair, so that the strands are taut. (When you lift the heddle, and push it down, the strands of yarn separate to create two different openings.)

CONTINUED

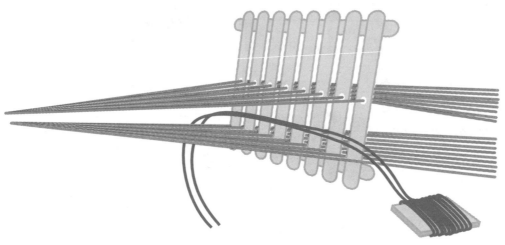

Popsicle-Stick Heddle Loom

Save the sticks from frozen treats and turn them into an ingenious heddle loom. You need 10 Popsicle sticks and a drill with an ⅛ inch (3 mm) bit. Drill a hole in the middle of 8 of the sticks. Assemble and glue the sticks to make a heddle like the one shown here.

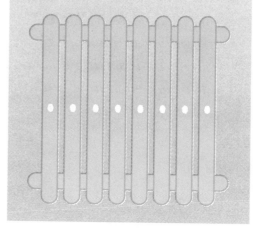

3. Double a length of yarn and wrap it around the cardboard. Lift the heddle and pass the doubled yarn through the opening in the strands. Now push the heddle down and pass the yarn back through the new opening. As you weave, pull the doubled yarn to bring the 17 strands together.

4. Continue in this way until the belt is the desired length. Cut the strands a few inches (about 10 cm) beyond the weaving, and tie them together in twos. Do the same at the beginning of the belt.

THE BEGINNING OF THE END

Historians divide the years that the Maya civilization existed into several stages. The greatest accomplishments were made during the so-called classic Maya phase, from around A.D. 250 to A.D. 900. Soon after that time, most of the important cultural centers were abandoned.

No one knows why communities that were once home to tens of thousands of people gradually became deserted. Some historians think overpopulation was the reason. Others believe a long drought, or dry spell, was responsible for making the people separate and move

elsewhere. Still others suspect hostile invaders sent them fleeing for their lives.

The heyday of the Maya may have come to an end, but pockets of nine major groups of Maya continue to make their home in Mexico. These descendants live in what are now the southern Mexican states Chiapas, Yucatán, Quintana Roo, and Campeche (as well as in neighboring Central American countries). Look at the map on page 6 and at your topo map to see the areas where this remarkable civilization existed in ancient times, and where descendants still live today.

Mexico: 1200 B.C.– A.D. 1800

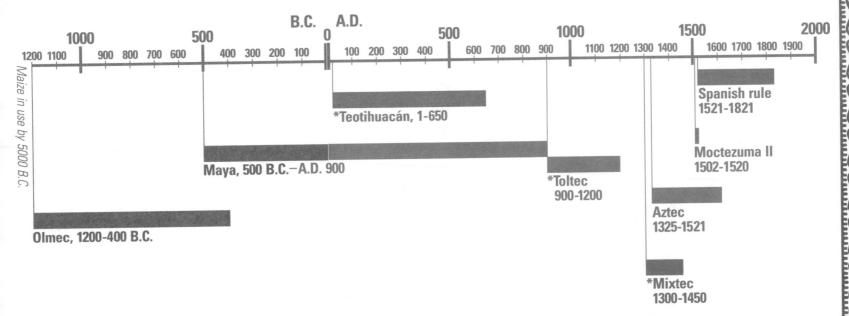

Maize in use by 5000 B.C.

Olmec, 1200-400 B.C.

Maya, 500 B.C.–A.D. 900

*Teotihuacán, 1-650

*Toltec 900-1200

*Mixtec 1300-1450

Aztec 1325-1521

Moctezuma II 1502-1520

Spanish rule 1521-1821

* other major ancient civilizations

THE AWESOME AZTEC

I magine a beautiful city, gleaming with white-washed stone buildings, complete with a zoo, towering pyramids, markets, and floating gardens where food and brightly colored flowers are grown. It sounds like a city anyone would delight in visiting today, but actually it was Tenochtitlán (ten-ohch-teet-LAHN), the Aztec capital city established in the early 1300s (see time line, page 53). Modern-day Mexico City sits atop the ruins of this once-great city.

Just who were the Aztec? Originally a wandering people from the north, the Aztec founded the last major ancient Mexican civilization — one that met its end at the hands of the conquering Spaniards in 1521. What is amazing is the speed with which the Aztec empire grew. In less than two hundred years, the Aztec ruled as many as six million people, including the peoples of many other Indian groups in surrounding areas. The capital city alone was home to more than two hundred thousand people, five times as large as London, England, at the time!

Map It!

Don't forget your topo map. Pick a color for the banners that will mark the borders of the Aztec empire (pages 6 and 29). Look at the topography (page 31) and decide if you think the location of the Aztec civilization had anything to do with its rise and fall.

FIRST-RATE BULLIES

How did the Aztec empire become so powerful in such a short time? In part, its leaders played upon the fears of people.

As in previous Mexican civilizations, religion played an all-important role in Aztec life. Every day, every night, each week, each month, and each year had its own god or goddess who needed to be pleased to prevent disaster. The ruling class used this powerful religious belief to manipulate the common people to do whatever the rulers asked — always done to honor or appease a god or goddess.

Aztec leaders didn't mind pushing others around, either! The Aztec battled and conquered many other native peoples and demanded they pay a special tax, called a tribute, to them. Among the things people brought to Tenochtitlán as tributes were food and salt, firewood, bags of cacao (cah-KAY-oh) beans (used to make chocolate), bunches of feathers, and a prized red dye made from the dried bodies of tiny insects.

THE BORROWERS

Like many Mexicans before them, the Aztec borrowed lots of ideas from the region's earlier peoples. Many of their beliefs about religion, human sacrifice, government, farming methods — to mention only a few aspects of Aztec life — had their origins in Olmec, Maya, and other cultures.

Huitzilopochtli warrior

The Aztec combined the many centuries of earlier learning with their own fierce determination. Encouraged by Huitzilopochtli (weetz-ill-oh-PACHT-lee) — their god of war, who was linked with the sun — they used their might to make themselves the greatest power in central Mexico at any time, before or since!

Think About It

Threats

The Aztec preyed upon people's fears to get power. In a teeny, tiny way we all have done that. "If you don't give me some candy, I'll tell Mom you had to stay after school." Sound somewhat familiar? How do threats make you feel? Are you more likely to do something if you are asked politely, or if you're threatened in some way?

A SPECIAL SNAKE

One of the first things the Aztec leaders needed to do as they traveled toward central Mexico was choose a place to settle down and build a capital.

As the story goes, the Aztec were on the lookout for an eagle perched on a prickly-pear cactus, dangling a snake from its mouth. The learned priests had said this would be the sign from Huitzilopochtli that they had found the ideal spot for their city. Did they actually find such a snake? We can't know for sure, but since the Aztec did finally settle in central Mexico, what do you think?

Design a Symbol

MEXICO TODAY

An Enduring Symbol

Today, the snake-eating eagle perched on a cactus is the symbol of Mexico. The image appears on the Mexican flag, on coins, paper money, and as a decoration.

When Mexico gained its independence from Spain in 1821, its leaders thought the 500-year-old Aztec symbol was a fitting one for their emerging nation.

Mexico's national symbol reminds Mexicans of one of the important cultures and times in their nation's past. Design a symbol for yourself — or your family, club, or school — that draws on some aspect of importance to you. If you admire strength and wisdom, perhaps you will draw a wise owl perched on a flexed arm.

Make a Toy Button Snake

Many different kinds of snakes — from rattlers to jungle vipers — are found in Mexico. There's even a popular toy snake made from wood. Its jointed body twists and turns just like a real snake's!

Make a similar twisty toy snake from buttons. Lay out a series of buttons in assorted sizes, starting with the smallest for the snake's tail, and working up in size for the body and head. Thread a needle with heavy buttonhole thread twice as long as the snake you wish to make, plus 6 inches (15 cm) or so.

Tie the end of the thread so that it won't pull out of the buttons, and then insert the needle through one hole in the largest button. Continue threading the buttons, until you reach the smallest. Now work your way back toward the head, inserting the needle through an opposite hole in each button. Tie the ends of the thread securely in a knot; trim it a short distance from the knot to make the snake's tongue.

THE "WRITE" STUFF

Several Spanish priests who came to Mexico in the early 1500s worked with the Aztec to write about their culture, before it was destroyed and disappeared forever.

Together, they created folding books known as codices (COH-deh-sees) that had been made for centuries. Some were made from tanned animal skin, others from paper made from the bark of a type of fig tree, or even the stringy strands of a desert plant called the maguey (mah-GAY).

Although the Spaniards destroyed many of the existing Aztec codices, a handful of the ones created with the help of the priests have survived. Today they can be found in several libraries and collections throughout the world.

Make a Codex

Make a codex (as a single folding book is called) to record something important to you, keep favorite drawings, or to give as a gift. It is sure to be treasured for a long time to come.

YOU WILL NEED:
- Narrow strips of paper
- Poster board or stiff paper
- Glue

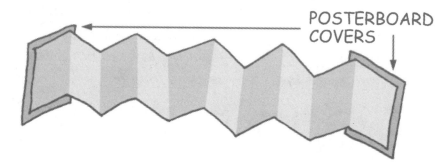

POSTERBOARD COVERS

1. Glue several strips of paper together to make one long strip. Fold this strip back and forth accordion-style to make the pages of your codex.

2. Cut two pieces of poster board just slightly larger than the folded paper. Glue a piece to each end of the paper strip.

Now you're ready to fill your codex with whatever you want! You can tell your story with pictures, symbols, or in a combination with words.

SMILING SUN

Like many of the Mexicans before them, the Aztec were worry warts. They worried when the sun shone hot for too long; they worried when rain clouds kept it hidden for too long. One of their greatest fears was that the sun would someday stop shining altogether, plunging the world into darkness and causing everything and everyone to die.

The Aztec believed it was necessary to provide the sun with "precious water" – human blood – to keep it shining. Prisoners taken from neighboring areas were killed and their hearts offered to the sun. In fact, this was the main reason for war – to capture people to be used as sacrifices. The Aztec believed these sacrifices were for the good of all, because without the sun there would be no life.

Demonstrate the Sun's Power

The Aztec awareness of the sun's power was well founded. See for yourself! Just what would happen if the sun beat down day after day without a break, or if it stopped shining altogether? It wouldn't be good, that's for sure!

Get an idea how the two extremes would affect the plant life on Earth with a simple experiment. You need three identical plants. Put a box or small paper bag over one plant. Place another plant a few inches from a fluorescent light, and leave the light on – night and day. Put the third plant in a sunny window. Water them all the same over a two- or three-week period.

How does lack of sunlight – or too much sunlight – affect the plants? Are you surprised?

HERE COMES THE SUN

With such importance placed on the sun in Mexico's past, it's not surprising that it has long been a popular theme in Mexican art.

Today, several types of Mexican folk art feature the sun. Among these are clay masks made in Metepec. The fired clay is given a coat of white paint, then decorated in dazzling shades of shocking colors.

The artisans in Oaxaca assemble items from cut and embossed tin using the sun motif — everything from tiny ornaments to frames for mirrors.

Make an Oaxacan-Style Sun Face

Make an Oaxacan-style sun face from materials you may already have at home. Tiny pie pans can be used to make ornaments to hang on a wall or window, or on a Christmas tree. Larger pie pans make good wall decorations.

1. Using scissors, cut a sun shape with rays from the pie pan.

2. Place on a folded dishtowel or cardboard, and draw designs all over the sun with the blunt pencil. Use just enough pressure to impress the aluminum without poking through it.

YOU WILL NEED:
- Scissors
- Aluminum pie pan
- Dishtowel or cardboard
- Blunt pencil
- Permanent markers
- Thin string

Note: Be sure to use permanent markers in a well-ventilated area. Wear old clothing, too.

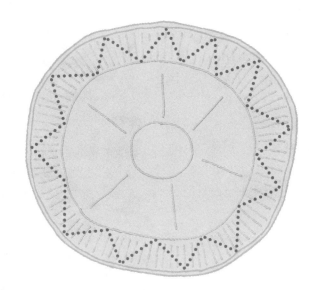

3. Turn the sun over (the "right" side is the side with the raised designs). Color the sun with permanent markers. Poke a hole in one of the rays, and attach a hanging string.

Make several and hang at different heights.

The 5 Worlds of the Aztec

Aztec myths describe the creation of five worlds, or ages, each destined to be destroyed by one of the awesome forces of nature — earth, wind, fire, and water.

◎ The first world was a place where giants roamed. The giants had not yet learned to farm, but still gathered the foods they ate. This world came to an end when a huge jaguar (earth) ate the giants.

◎ The second world didn't fare much better. This world was inhabited by a smaller number of people, but it was destroyed by hurricanes (wind). The few surviving people were turned into monkeys.

◎ The third world ended in fire. The people who managed to escape flew into the sky as birds.

◎ The fourth world disappeared when rains (water) flooded the earth. Those people who didn't drown became fish.

◎ The fifth world — the present world — saw the creation of the sun, the moon, and human beings as we know them. The Aztec believed this world would also come to a terrible end, like the others before it. How? Hang on! It's predicted to end in earthquakes!

SUN STONE

A giant — 12 feet (4 m) in diameter — carved stone disk, known as the Sun Stone, adorned the Temple of Huitzilopochtli in Tenochtitlán. Once believed to be a calendar, the stone actually shows the four elements — earth, wind, fire, and water — which the Aztec believed destroyed four previous "worlds." In the very center is a face that most probably represents the sun god.

Buried by the conquering Spaniards in the 1500s, the stone was unearthed in 1790. Its discovery was a turning point in Mexican cultural pride. It made the Mexican people want to know more about their native heritage. Today it hangs in the National Museum of Anthropology in Mexico City, where it's admired by thousands of visitors each year.

SHAKE, RATTLE, AND ROLL

The sun wasn't the only thing the Aztec worried about. They also fretted when the earth shook. Because Mexico lies where three of the earth's plates (rigid pieces of its crust) meet, it has many earthquakes, especially where the two mountain chains running along the coasts meet in the central part of the country. (Look at your topo map, as well as the maps, pages 5 and 31.)

While most tremors are mild, Mexico has suffered its share of earthquake disasters. One of the most devastating took place in September, 1985, when a violent quake shook Mexico City, killing nearly ten thousand people, leaving thirty thousand injured, and at least ninety-five thousand more homeless.

The Two Lovers

Mexicans tell a story about the volcanoes they call Ixta and Popo, found just outside Mexico City. This is one version of the tender tale.

There once was an Indian princess named Ixtaccíhuatl (Ixta) who loved kind, gentle Popocatépetl (Popo) and hoped to someday marry him. Ixta's father, however, insisted that Popo first prove himself a worthy warrior. While Popo was away fighting, other young men called on the princess, hoping to persuade her to marry one of them instead.

Ixta was determined to wait for Popo's return, but one sly suitor convinced her that her beloved had died in battle. Brokenhearted, the princess wandered to the top of a mountain, where she lay down and wept. It began to snow, but Ixta did not even notice. It snowed and snowed, until the princess's body was completely covered, and her cries could no longer be heard.

When Popo returned and learned that Ixta's sleeping body had turned to stone on the mountaintop, he scaled a nearby peak where he could watch over her. The snow blanketed his body as he, too, took on the shape of a mountain. The two lovers — transformed into Mexico's best-loved volcanoes — can be seen to this day.

ONE FOR ME ... ONE FOR ME!

The ancient Mexicans were crazy about chocolate. Cacao beans, the seeds from which cocoa and chocolate are made, were once so highly valued that they were actually used like money. In fact, the success of the ancient Maya civilization was thought to be due to trade in cacao beans.

The Aztec drank great quantities of a bitter beverage made from this special bean. It wasn't something they shared with their children, though! It was a sacred drink, and only men of superior rank — priests, warlords, and other members of the ruling class — were allowed to drink the bitter brew.

Think About It

Throughout history, different items of value have been used as money — from cacao beans to gold. If you were in charge, what would you use as money?

THEN & NOW Mexican chocolate has a grainy texture, thanks to the addition of ground almonds, cinnamon, cloves, and vanilla. While it is used to make a hot beverage, it is also used as an ingredient in cooking. Mexico's national dish, *mole poblano* (MOH-lay poh-BLAH-noh), a rich and spicy chile sauce, counts chocolate among its many ingredients!

YUM—MEXICAN HOT CHOCOLATE!

It was said that Moctezuma II, the Aztec ruler at the time of the Spanish conquest, drank 50 cups of chocolate, served in a solid gold cup, each day!

Treat yourself like royalty and whip up a steaming cup of chocolate with a very different flavor. Look for Mexican chocolate in the imported foods section of your supermarket. If you can't find it, use semi-sweet chocolate instead, adding ¼ teaspoon (1.5 ml) ground cinnamon to give it a hint of that special Mexican flavor.

Then, grate or crush 1 ounce (28 g) chocolate, and add it to ¾ cup (175 ml) milk in a small saucepan. With a grown-up's help, warm over low heat, stirring occasionally.

When the chocolate has melted, whisk it until it's nice and frothy. Pour into a mug. Makes one serving.

Swizzle Stick

THEN & NOW For centuries, Mexicans have been whipping their hot chocolate with a wooden tool called a *molinillo* (moh-lin-EE-yoh). Still used today, the hand-carved stick is rapidly twirled between outstretched palms to give the hot milk a frothy head.

ONE, TWO, THREE: STIR, STIR, CHOCOLATE!

Here's a popular finger play that mimics whipping hot chocolate to a froth. Recite the words while making your own hot drink.

Uno, dos, tres, cho- [count with fingers]
Uno, dos, tres, -co-
Uno, dos, tres, -la-
Uno, dos, tres, -te.
Bate, bate chocolate. (BAH-tay, BAH-tay, cho-coh-LAH-tay)
[rub hands back and forth as if using a molinillo]

¡VIVA LOS MEXICANOS!

Moctezuma II

When the Spanish began their invasion of Mexico in 1519, the Aztec were ruled by an emperor named Moctezuma II. As a young man, Moctezuma was a warrior who helped conquer the Aztec's neighbors. Later, he became a rich and powerful leader.

Like many peoples around the world, the Aztec believed that their rulers also had important religious roles to play — Moctezuma was like a general, a president, and a priest all rolled into one!

In the years before the Spanish arrived, many strange things happened in Moctezuma's realm: There was a drought, lightning struck a sacred temple in Tenochtitlán, and a comet appeared in the skies. No wonder Moctezuma thought the gods were trying to warn him about something!

Because of this, and an Aztec legend telling how one of their gods, Quetzalcóatl, would appear on the eastern ocean, Moctezuma didn't attack the Spanish when they first arrived. He wasn't sure who they were. Could they be messengers from Quetzalcóatl?

Moctezuma played it safe. He gave the Spanish gifts of gold and invited them to Tenochtitlán, but when they arrived there, they took him prisoner in his own palace.

The Spanish later said that the Aztec killed Moctezuma by throwing stones at him; the Aztec said that the Spanish killed the emperor when he failed to stop his angry subjects from revolting. One thing for sure, this Aztec ruler was between a rock and a hard place!

THE FALL OF THE AZTEC

As fate would have it, the very traits that made the Aztec empire grow so rapidly were to be its undoing. Remember those bullying leaders? Well, many of the native peoples under Aztec control were tired of being pushed around by them. When the Spanish came ashore in 1519, they quickly sized up the situation and encouraged these unhappy native peoples to help. Thus, the hated Aztec empire was toppled, and within two years, the Spaniards took over the region.

OLD WORLD MEETS NEW

The year was 1519. Hernán Cortés (air-NAHN core-TESS) and his Spanish soldiers arrived in Tenochtitlán, the Aztec capital located in central Mexico. Two very different cultures — each having developed for thousands of years with absolutely no knowledge of the other — suddenly came face to face. Imagine the cultural shock!

What was the result of this meeting? Enormous changes, especially for the inhabitants of the New World, as Mexico and the rest of the Americas came to be known. The Spaniards brought with them many things from the Old World — from fabulous customs to dreaded diseases — that would forever change the face of Mexico.

ON HER MAJESTY'S MISSION

Just what were the Spaniards doing so far from home when they set foot on Mexican soil in the early 1500s? The answer rests with Christopher Columbus.

When Columbus "discovered" the New World in 1492, he was on a royal mission for Queen Isabella of Spain. He was hoping to find precious metals for her, such as gold and silver, as well as valuable spices such as cinnamon, cloves, and black pepper. He never found what he was searching for, but other Spaniards made similar voyages. Eventually colonies were established in the Caribbean, where native peoples were treated like slaves.

Because the Caribbean natives had no natural immunities to European diseases, many of them died. It was while searching for other people to enslave that Hernán Cortés and his soldiers first set foot on Mexican soil.

A GREAT LOSS

When Cortés and his men arrived in Tenochtitlán in 1519, were they ever impressed! Here was an incredibly beautiful city, filled with riches and wonders beyond belief. But, the Spaniards were also disgusted by many of the culture's customs — particularly by the human sacrifices — which they saw as proof that the Aztec were godless people.

In an attempt to erase everything that had to do with Aztec culture, Cortés had all the buildings and everyday objects demolished. Then, Christian churches and other buildings that reflected the Spanish culture were constructed on top of the rubble from the destruction of Tenochtitlán.

Think About It

Give Peace a Chance

Was there any chance at all that the Spaniards and the Aztec could have lived and worked together when these two cultures came upon one another? What might the future have been like if peaceful coexistence had actually occurred?

MEXICO TODAY

Tenochtitlán Uncovered

Over the years, as land has been cleared for new construction in Mexico City, bits and pieces of Aztec architecture and artifacts have been uncovered. Portions of Aztec buildings can be viewed throughout the city — some even in Metro, or subway, stations. It's a striking example of how close Mexico's past and present truly are!

Dig for Treasure

Hard Choices

Mexico is not the only place where pieces of our human past are hidden just beneath our feet.

In Athens, Greece, a meeting of the past and present has caused a serious dilemma: A new subway system is being installed to reduce car traffic pollutants that are destroying the city's ancient ruins. But, the subway construction is destroying rare archaeological finds underground!

What would you do? Save what's above ground (and lose a huge portion of the world's ancient archaeological history) or save what's below ground (and lose the world's treasured Acropolis and Parthenon)? Can you think of any win-win options?

Thinking like an archaeologist, what can you discover about the people who once called your house "home"? Dig carefully for treasure outside your home (be sure to get permission first!). Can you find any small items buried in the ground — pieces of pottery, marbles and other toys, or hair barrettes and jewelry? Do any of your finds tell you if a family, an elderly person, a dog or cat, or a boy or a girl lived in your house?

Hunt for treasure inside your home, too. Are there initials carved in the wood in the attic or printed in cement in the basement? Are there markings in the closet that look like growth charts for the kids? Are there places, such as behind radiators and near fireplace chimneys, where things could have fallen and been forgotten? The walls in some of the rooms in your home may be covered by wallpaper, even several layers. Ask permission to peel back the different layers in a closet or other out-of-the-way spot. What can you learn about changing tastes in decorating?

Share your finds and hunches with others in the house, and see if you can re-create an idea of who lived there and what they were like.

"Calavera" by José Posada

THE GRIM REAPER

The Spanish arrival on Mexican shores meant the introduction of European diseases. Like the Caribbean natives before them, many Mexicans became sick and died from mild childhood diseases like chicken pox, measles, and mumps. That's because these diseases were new to the Mexicans, and they hadn't developed any immunities, or natural protections, against them.

Disease wasn't the only killer. Many enslaved Mexicans died from overwork and mistreatment. Others tried hiding from the Spaniards, fleeing to remote regions. Too afraid to settle in one place, for fear they would be captured, these people could not grow the crops they needed for food, and died from hunger.

Nearly 90 percent of the native peoples of Mexico died within one hundred years of the Spaniards' arrival! People in all walks of life, from the ruling classes to the lowliest slaves, were affected. Mexico would never be the same; the country and its people were devastated.

Think About It

When Will We Learn?

If everything you knew, believed, possessed, and cared about were suddenly forbidden or taken away, what would be the one thing you would miss the most? Would it be the loss of a person, or a place? A belief? A freedom?

Unfortunately, this is not so far-fetched an idea. This destruction of people and their belief systems has repeated itself throughout human history right up to today. Interestingly, this kind of purge most commonly is done in the name of religion! Does that make any sense to you?

UNDERSTANDING PERCENTAGES

Per cent (%) is Latin for "in every hundred." Saying that 90 percent of Mexicans died from disease or mistreatment within the first 100 years of Spanish rule means that 90 out of every 100 people died during that time.

When we talk of percentages, we use 100 to mean "all." If, for example, you ate 100 percent of your dinner, you ate all of it. Say you didn't like dinner, and your mom said, "Eat half and then you can have dessert." If you did as she suggested, you would have eaten 50 percent of your dinner (as half of 100 is 50).

THE CATHOLIC CHURCH

The Spanish colonists brought their particular branch of Christianity, known as Roman Catholicism, to Mexico. They were determined to convert, or change, the Aztec to this religion. When the Aztec saw the miserable consequences of not conforming to this new religion, they appeared to embrace it. But, of course, it wasn't as simple as that.

detail from "The New Messiah" by José Posada

RACE RELATIONS

Mexico's population began to grow, as native peoples and Spaniards married and started their own families.

For many years, the *mestizos* (mess-TEE-sohs), or people of mixed Spanish and native parentage, were scorned by the ruling Spaniards. Only much later did the mestizos begin to celebrate their unique heritage. Today, the majority of Mexicans are mestizos.

What about the rest of today's Mexicans? A small percentage are pure Indians who trace their ancestry to the native peoples who settled the country thousands of years ago. An even smaller number of Mexicans are of pure Spanish ancestry, which means that generation after generation of these people married only other people of Spanish descent. Their great-great-great-great-and-more grandparents may be among the Spaniards who colonized Mexico nearly five hundred years ago! (See page 33 to figure out exactly how many "greats" belong here.)

¡VIVA LOS MEXICANOS!

Sister Juana Inés de la Cruz

In 1651, Juana Santillana was born in a small village outside Mexico City. When she was a little girl, she loved to learn more than anything. She spent most of her time reading books, and, later, writing plays and poems.

When Juana Santillana was only 17 years old, she decided to become a Catholic nun, but her reading and writing got her into trouble! People believed women, especially nuns, should not read books and write poems. Sister Inés de la Cruz wasn't afraid to stick up for the rights of all women to be educated and say what they believed.

To this day, Sister Inés de la Cruz's poetry and courage are cherished not only by Mexicans, but by all Americans and people around the world.

DÍA DE LA RAZA

October 12 (what North Americans call Columbus Day) is celebrated in Mexico as *Día de la Raza* (DEE-ah day lah ORAH-sah), or Race Day. It honors the people of mixed Spanish and native Mexican heritage. On this day, fiestas are held with plenty of delicious food, dancing, and of course, music!

"Popular Dance Hall" by José Posada

A NEW ORDER

The structure of society changed when the Spaniards took over Mexico. Suddenly, the Spaniards were the ruling class.

Below them came their descendants – people whose parents were Spanish, but who were themselves born in Mexico. Known as *criollos* (cree-OH-yohs), they were considered second-class citizens. Further down on the ladder were *mestizos*, people of mixed Spanish and Indian or mixed black and Indian blood. At the very bottom were the original inhabitants of Mexico, the various groups of native peoples, who were called *indios*, or Indians, by the Spaniards. Does this make sense to you?

Think About It

Not everyone thinks *Día de la Raza* is a day for celebration. For some, this is a reminder of how badly native peoples — not only in the Americas, but all over the world — have been treated by those who conquered, or colonized, them. Others are torn between their feelings of pride for their new race and anger about being colonized and forced to submit to another culture. Still others are reminded of how poorly minorities are treated around the world.

It's a very complicated issue. What are some ways to honor the past and move forward, together, in the present?

WE, THE PEOPLE

Mexico's native peoples are sometimes referred to as *indios* — a term many feel is unflattering. They would prefer to be called by the names they call themselves. The Lacondón Maya who live in the rainforest of Chiapas, for example, call themselves *hach uinik*, or "true people."

THE CRY FOR INDEPENDENCE

The Spanish ruled Mexico for nearly three hundred years, during which time people — especially native Mexicans — suffered. In 1810, Miguel Hidalgo y Costilla, a priest, began to raise interest in gaining independence. In his speech, *Grito de Dolores*, or Cry of Dolores (a city), Hidalgo inspired a gathering crowd to form an army to make conditions better for the poor majority. He was executed 11 years before Mexico was freed from Spanish rule in 1821. Yet, it is Hidalgo who is considered the "father of Mexican independence." He is remembered each year on Mexican Independence Day, September 16. Yes, Hidalgo is proof that one person can make a huge difference.

"My children, a new dispensation comes to us this day. Are you ready to receive it? Will you be free? Will you make the effort to recover from the hated Spaniards the lands stolen from your forefathers three hundred years ago?"

"Mexicans! Long live Mexico!"

— **Miguel Hidalgo y Costilla, an excerpt from *Cry of Dolores***

CHECK IT OUT

You may be of mixed ancestry yourself — in fact, most everyone is! Find out by asking your parents or grandparents about their heritage.

The older our world gets, the more the heritage stew gets mixed. Doesn't this make you wonder why people aren't more accepting of others? After all, the "others" may very well be part of them, too!

Mexico: Recent History (1800-2000)

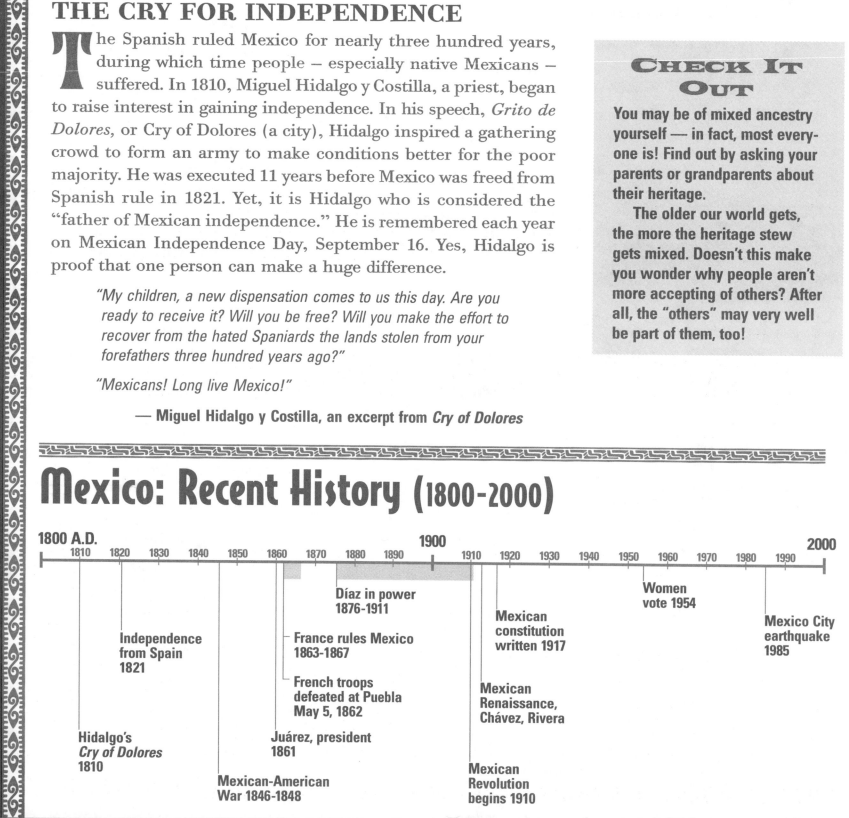

1800 A.D. — 1810 1820 1830 1840 1850 1860 1870 1880 1890 — 1900 — 1910 1920 1930 1940 1950 1960 1970 1980 1990 — 2000

Hidalgo's Cry of Dolores 1810

Independence from Spain 1821

Mexican-American War 1846-1848

Juárez, president 1861

French troops defeated at Puebla May 5, 1862

France rules Mexico 1863-1867

Díaz in power 1876-1911

Mexican Revolution begins 1910

Mexican Renaissance, Chávez, Rivera

Mexican constitution written 1917

Women vote 1954

Mexico City earthquake 1985

MEXICAN-AMERICAN WAR

The trouble between Mexico and the United States began when Texas, then a part of Mexico, declared its independence in 1835, leading to the famous Battle of the Alamo. Keep in mind, from the Mexican point of view, Texas rightfully belonged to Mexico. Then, in 1845, Texas joined the United States, which was also trying to obtain modern-day New Mexico and California, both part of Mexico at that time.

As you can imagine, none of this pleased Mexico. Then, a small fight broke out between Mexican and United States troops, leading the United States to declare war against Mexico in 1846.

Within two years, the United States (which had more money and better-trained troops) captured Mexico City and won the war. Mexico was reduced to half its size, forced to sell its northern territories (see map, page 7) to the United States for only $18 million. It's no surprise that Mexico didn't feel very friendly towards the United States, for many years to come.

¡VIVA LOS MEXICANOS!

Benito Pablo Juárez

Benito Pablo Juárez, born in 1806, is one of Mexico's most famous leaders. Coming from a poor Zapotec Indian family, Juárez had to work hard to educate himself; he even went to several different schools looking for one that would do the best job!

He was active in the Mexican-American War, and the Mexican Civil War, becoming president of Mexico in 1861, and again in 1867.

To this day, Benito Juárez is remembered as a man who lived simply and tried to do one thing above all else: Make life better for all the people of Mexico. As he once said: "Let the people and government respect the rights of all — among individuals as among nations, peace is respect for the rights of others."

UNDER FRENCH RULE

In the middle of the 19th century, Mexico was going through a difficult economic period. The government had borrowed money from other countries, but was unable to pay it back. One of the lending nations was France. At that time, France was ruled by Napoleon III who decided to attempt a take-over of Mexico, rather than try to get his country's money back. French troops attacked but were successfully defeated on May 5, 1862 (commemorated each year as *Cinco de Mayo*). The French, however, did overtake Mexico the following year.

France appointed Ferdinand Maximilian as emperor of Mexico in 1864. He and his wife, Carlota, were not strong leaders, but they left their mark on Mexico (the wide boulevards in Mexico City and French bread rolls are still enjoyed to this day!). The French reign ended in 1867, when Maximilian was executed by Mexicans.

¡CINCO DE MAYO!

For many Mexicans, and Mexican-Americans, *Cinco de Mayo*, or the Fifth of May, is a time to celebrate Latino culture, Mexican unity, and patriotism.

The date marks the incredible victory of the Mexican army and citizens of Puebla, over the French on May 5, 1862. Armed with little more than farming tools, this brave group of people held back an army three times its size – many say out of sheer determination! It was an army peopled by the new and old Mexicans, fighting together for a common cause – their country's survival!

"The Fifth of May" by José Posada

Cook Up Some Menudo

A traditional Cinco de Mayo *treat enjoyed by many Mexicans is* menudo *(men-OO-thoh), a hearty soup flavored with tripe (beef stomach). You can make a quick-to-fix version ... without the tripe!*

Ask a grown-up to help you assemble these ingredients in a saucepan: 1 quart (1 L) beef broth, 1 can whole white hominy, 1 can chopped green chiles, ¼ chopped onion, 1 minced clove garlic, 1 teaspoon (5 ml) oregano, 2 peppercorns, and a pinch of salt. Let simmer for ½ hour; then, serve in shallow bowls with salsa and fresh tortillas (see pages 21 and 23 for these recipes).

REVOLUTION!

From 1876 to 1911, Mexico was governed by a dictator, Porfirio Díaz (por-FEE-ree-oh DEE-ahs). During this time, the gap between rich and poor grew very wide. Half of Mexico's rural population worked like slaves for a handful of wealthy landowners. Factory and mine workers were treated just as poorly.

Before long, the workers rebelled, but change came slowly. One in eight Mexicans was killed during the revolutionary battles of 1910-20. In 1911, President Diaz fell from power. Several years later, a new constitution was drafted that continues to define the laws and rights of the people of Mexico to this day! It called for free education, limited church powers, curbed foreign investments, and set forth labor and land reforms.

¡VIVA LOS MEXICANOS!

Emiliano Zapata

One of the most famous people to fight in the Mexican Revolution was Emiliano Zapata. Like many farmers, Zapata grew angry as the rich land owners took more and more from working Mexicans like himself.

In 1909, the villagers elected Zapata to present their problems to the local government, but he was ignored. When the revolution broke out, Zapata organized his followers into a small army called the Zapatistas.

To some, Zapata was just a bandit, but to many Mexicans, he was a hero fighting for their rights. Zapata's slogan became *Tierra y Libertad*, "Land and Freedom."

Emiliano Zapata

FOR ALL TO SEE

In the early 1900s, the Mexican people used more than words to communicate their feelings about government and social changes. Many artists used their creativity to stir people's consciences about Mexico's past and present. A favorite medium of expression was the mural, a giant painting created in a public space.

From the 1920s through the 1950s, Diego Rivera, José Clemente Orozco, and David Alfaro Siqueiros – "The Big Three," as they are known – created many important murals. Their massive paintings tell about the history and social problems of their home country.

On Display

Do any of the public buildings in your area have murals? You may discover both interior murals (in banks, town halls, or theaters) and exterior ones (look on the sides of buildings near schools, universities, and city halls). What was the artist saying?

¡VIVA LOS MEXICANOS!

detail of Rivera mural from "Escuela national de agricultura"

Diego Rivera

Remember Carlos Chávez and the Mexican Renaissance (page 16)? Like Carlos Chávez, Diego Rivera thought it was important for Mexican art to reach back and touch the spirit of Mexico's ancient peoples. He also saw that his art could become a voice for the poor people of Mexico, whom the government often seemed to ignore. At one point, Rivera called himself "a revolutionary with a paintbrush."

In the 1920s and 1930s, Rivera painted many of his famous murals in Mexico and the United States. In these works, he told the story of Mexico — of its diverse peoples and ideas — to other Mexicans, as well as to the people of the world!

Paint a Mural

YOU WILL NEED:
- Paper
- Pencil
- Ruler
- Paint
- Paintbrushes

Use your artistic creativity to make a statement about something that concerns you. Use color and shape to communicate your message boldly. Will you use symbolism or capture reality on your mural? Will your mural communicate in story fashion or with one stark image?

Think "simple" and "bold" when designing your mural. Too much fussy detail makes a mural hard to interpret when viewed from a distance. Experiment with unusual angles and colors to make it both eye-catching and thought-provoking.

Paint your mural on long paper (like butcher paper), working up a small-scale drawing first, then, enlarging it (see below). Then, tack it to the wall.

Big, Bigger, Biggest

Here's an easy way to enlarge artwork. With a ruler, mark an even grid of squares onto the drawing you wish to make bigger. Now, draw a grid of larger squares onto a larger piece of paper. Working one square at a time, transfer the lines in each of the smaller squares to the larger ones. You'll end up with the same drawing, only bigger!

¡VIVA LOS MEXICANOS!

Frida Kahlo

Frida Kahlo had polio when she was 6 years old. Even after she got better, she had trouble walking, so the other kids picked on her and called her names.

Then, when she was 18 years old, she was in a bus accident that left her seriously hurt. It was while she was recovering, stuck in her bedroom, that she started to paint. At one point, she showed some of her work to Diego Rivera; he liked it and they became friends, eventually getting married!

Frida Kahlo loved Mexico and its people. She showed that joy through her paintings and by wearing traditional Mexican clothes. There were tough times in her life, so a lot of Kahlo's art expresses the sadness and bitterness she felt. Whether happy or sad, the art of this Mexican woman is highly respected around the world!

LOOKING FOR A BETTER LIFE

Though millions of people live happy lives in Mexico, each year thousands try to leave the country – often illegally.

This doesn't happen just in Mexico, of course. People the world over often leave a beloved homeland in search of a better life for themselves and their children. Just remember what brought the boatloads of pilgrims to the United States in 1620.

Think About It

Mexicans who enter the United States without permission or proper papers are breaking the law. Known as illegal aliens, most are honest people desperate to work to provide food and shelter for their families.

What do you think you would do if you weren't able to find work to support your family in your own country, yet you lived near one where there were many opportunities? Would you risk being punished (or even killed) so that you could work there?

KEEPING THE FAITH

For nearly 500 years, communities throughout Mexico have been built up around the Catholic Church – literally! A church is found in every town and village, no matter how small. The buildings themselves and the many teachings that are a part of Catholicism bring the people of Mexico together daily.

Catholicism was introduced into Mexico in the early 1500s, when the Spaniards colonized the region. Of course, the Aztec and other Mexican peoples already worshipped their own gods. They were forced to give these up by the conquering Spanish and accept a completely unknown religion. Were they able to do this? Well, there was partial acceptance, although many people continued to keep their age-old beliefs, as you might expect.

THE BEGINNING OF THE CHURCH

After destroying Aztec temples and other places of worship, the Spanish colonists set about establishing churches and schools to teach Catholicism.

The Spanish quickly realized that if some of the Aztec symbols were mixed in with Catholicism – for instance, by allowing the Aztec sun god to represent the Christian God – the Aztec would be more inclined to accept the new religion.

Very gradually, over several hundred years, Catholicism took hold. Today, most Mexicans are Catholic. But, many church rituals, like other customs in Mexico, result from a unique blending of ancient pagan traditions and the Catholic rituals imported from Spain.

A SPECIAL LADY

A vision of the Virgin of Guadalupe before the eyes of an Aztec man in December, 1531, was an important event in converting the Aztec to Catholicism.

As one version of the story goes, the ghostlike figure of the Virgin Mary appeared before Juan Diego, who had recently become a Christian (and taken a Spanish name). She asked Juan to tell the bishop of Mexico to build a shrine in her honor on a certain site.

"Our Lady the Virgin of Guadalupe" by José Posada

MEXICO TODAY

Other Faiths

While the vast majority of people in Mexico are Catholic, other religions are represented throughout the country. A very small percentage of Mexicans are practicing Jews, Muslims, and Buddhists. An even smaller percentage participate in other Christian religions such as Protestant, Lutheran, and Baptist.

When Juan went to see the bishop, the holy man asked for proof of the Virgin's existence. On December 12, Juan returned to the place he'd first seen the Virgin. There she was again, only this time she asked Juan to take some roses to the bishop. Not only did Juan bring roses — astounding everyone because roses did not bloom that time of year — but when he opened his cloak to show them to the bishop, an image of the Virgin was visible on his garment's cloth.

Thus, the Lady of Guadalupe became the patron saint of Mexico, and eventually, a shrine was built for her in Mexico City.

WHEN THE SAINTS GO MARCHING IN

Mexicans (and Roman Catholics in other countries) honor many saints, or people who were outstanding Christians. Many saints have "feast days" when they are remembered. True to their name, feast days often involve the preparation of special foods.

Some saints' days are especially fun for kids. The feast day of St. Anthony – the patron saint of animals – on January 17 is one of these. On this day, children throughout Mexico dress their farm animals and pets. Doll clothes are put on smaller animals, but even cows, horses, and sheep wear hats or are decorated with garlands of flowers! Then, it's off to the local church, where the village priest blesses the animals.

Think About It

Throughout history, people from many different faiths have not been free to practice the religion of their choice. How would you and your family continue to observe the important rituals of your religion if they were against the law?

Make a Tree of Life Candleholder

The Tree of Life, or Arbol de la Vida, *represents the apple tree in the biblical Garden of Eden. The image is found in many places in Mexican life, from woven blankets to tinware to pottery candleholders. Some of the most decorative are the brightly painted candelabras made by potters in the state of Puebla.*

Make your own Tree of Life candleholder. Decorate it with birds and flowers, or include tiny figures that have special meaning to you.

Please note: Be sure to light and burn candles under adult supervision only!

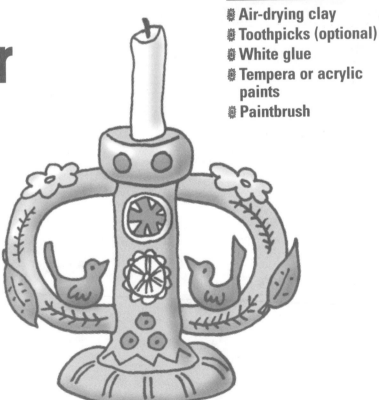

YOU WILL NEED:

- Air-drying clay
- Toothpicks (optional)
- White glue
- Tempera or acrylic paints
- Paintbrush

CONTINUED

1. Make the trunk of the tree by rolling some clay into a cylinder about 1 inch (2.5 cm) in diameter and 6 inches (15 cm) long.

Form a piece of clay into a rounded base. Moisten one end of the trunk and carefully push it down onto the base. (If the trunk is wobbly, reinforce it by sticking some toothpicks through the base into the trunk.)

More Alike than Different

The Tree of Life is a part of the lore of people all over the world. In Scandinavian mythology, the tree is called Yggdrasil *(IG-druh-sill)*. The gods supposedly met under this great ash tree each day to decide important matters.

On Sumatra (a large island in Indonesia), each leaf of the Tree of Life has a word written on it, such as "wealth," "happiness," and so on. The Sumatrans say the soul of each newborn child picks a leaf that then determines that child's future.

How do you think such different cultures came to all have a Tree of Life?

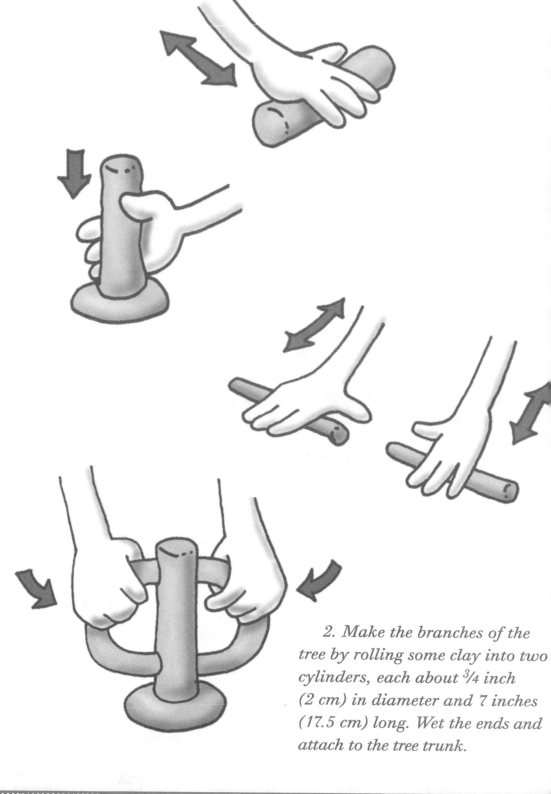

2. Make the branches of the tree by rolling some clay into two cylinders, each about ¾ inch (2 cm) in diameter and 7 inches (17.5 cm) long. Wet the ends and attach to the tree trunk.

3. Form a small ball of clay into a holder for a birthday-size candle. Attach to the top of the trunk. Make assorted figures, such as simple flowers, leaves, and birds, and attach them to the candlestick, wherever you would like.

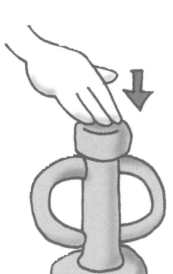

4. Let the clay thoroughly dry (this may take several days). Reattach any small parts that may have fallen off with glue. Paint designs with bright colors.

Note: You might also like to make a bigger Tree of Life by building a form out of wire, sticks, or pieces of wood, inserted into a Styrofoam or clay base. Cover the form with recycled pieces of foil or papier-mâché, and attach decorations with glue.

THE MAYA TREE OF LIFE

The ancient Maya imagined the world as a flat square held up at each of its four corners by bearded gods called Bacabs. Beneath them, in the underworld, stood four figures who kept the earth steady. In the very center was the Tree of Life, whose roots went down into the underworld and whose branches touched the heavens. The Maya say that earthquakes are the result of each god shifting his weight of the earth to the next god.

MIRACLE OF MIRACLES

Mexicans, like many, turn to prayer when they or someone they know becomes ill. A person might pray to a particular saint to help cure the ailment or ease the suffering.

When sick people recover or are cured of a disease, they often purchase a small tin decoration known as a *milagro* (mee-LAH-gro), or miracle. (Someone who survived a heart attack would buy a heart-shaped milagro.) This is pinned to the saint's statue in the local church as a thank you.

Make a *Milagro*

Make a milagro in the shape of something that reminds you of what you're thankful for. Then, place it in a window, hang it from the rear-view mirror of your car, or offer it to a special person as a thank you!

Make your milagro from aluminum cut from a pie tin. Cut out the shape of your milagro with a small pair of scissors. Use a blunt pencil to draw details on the shape. Poke a small hole in

the milagro, and tie a thread through it for hanging. Or, if you like, attach a safety pin to the back so that you can wear the milagro like a pin.

Do You Believe?

Many people believe in miracles, especially those who have had extraordinary things happen to them. Think about a time that something wonderful and inexplicable happened to you. Do you think it was a miracle or something else?

DEARLY DEPARTED

Every year on November 1 and 2, Mexicans remember deceased family members with a celebration known as *el Día de los Muertos* (el DEE-ah day lohs MWAIR-tohs), or the Day of the Dead. Like many Mexican celebrations, it is a blend of ancient Indian traditions and Catholic customs.

The native peoples of Mexico believed that the dead returned once a year to be fed, and so special feasts were prepared for them. In the Aztec calendar, this ritual fell around midsummer.

The Spanish priests combined this tradition with two European customs: observing All Saints' Day on November 1, when all of the saints who don't have their own feast day are honored; and All Souls' Day on November 2, a time for remembering everyone else who had died. The Mexican and European traditions gradually merged into an annual Day of the Dead celebration that is uniquely Mexican.

"La calavera catrina" by José Posada

DID YOU KNOW?

The Maya celebrated October 30 as a special day for remembering children who had died. They believed little children came back for the night and so prepared treats and decorations especially for them.

More Alike than Different

Most cultures set aside a special time to remember deceased family and friends. The Japanese honor the dead during a three-day festival called Obon. Lanterns are lit to guide the spirits home, where a place is set at the table for any family members who have recently died.

In Nepal, during the "Cow Festival," families with a death in the past year decorate a cow and let it loose to wander in the streets. They do this because it is believed that cows open the gate of heaven with their horns.

What other customs do you know that honor the dead?

THE ART OF THE DEAD

Art featuring skeletons has been made in Mexico for thousands of years. It seems Mexicans have been viewing death as a natural part of life for a very long time! More recently, in 1989, the acclaimed folk artist Josefina Aguilar created a wonderful ceramic sculpture, called "Laughing Skeletons."

detail from "Calavera" by José Posada

More Alike than Different

This time of year is a "sweet" one for kids in the U.S., too. Candy, after all, is a big part of Halloween!

Like el Día de los Muertos, Halloween is an ancient pagan celebration. It traces its roots to Great Britain, where it has been celebrated for at least two thousand years. On this day, ancient Britons (people who lived in England) believed the souls of the dead returned to Earth. But, they also anticipated lots of mischief at this time, and masks were used to scare away witches and hobgoblins!

THE HAPPY FACE OF DEATH

For weeks leading up to November, marketplaces throughout Mexico are filled with skulls and skeletons, made in every size, shape, and material imaginable. Edible skulls are found in sweet shops and bakeries. There are skeleton piñatas and glazed pottery skulls. Grinning wire skeletons play musical instruments, ride bicycles, and dangle their bony legs from astride burros.

Inside homes, families prepare shrines in memory of loved ones who have died. A shrine can be as simple as a photo and some mementos propped on a shelf. More elaborate shrines are decorated with skull and skeleton figurines, marigolds (the traditional Day of the Dead flower), and heaping platters of food. The food is believed to "feed" the dead person for one year.

Come nightfall, cemeteries all over Mexico are transformed into festive playgrounds. Crowds of people proceed by flickering candlelight to the graves of their loved ones. After offering prayers, everyone feasts on the food they've brought. Now, what do you think about that as a way to honor the dead?

Make a Candy Skull

Candy skulls are sold in shops and on street corners for several weeks before the Day of the Dead. Many have names on them, written in icing or on a piece of attached paper. Make your own candy skulls to give as Halloween gifts, for a Mexican-style celebration, or to eat all by yourself!

All you need is an almond paste called marzipan (check the baking section of your supermarket), brightly colored icing that comes in a tube, and candy decorations. Shape a piece of marzipan into a skull. Use a toothpick or small knife to make hollows for the eyes and nose, and draw a grinning mouth. Decorate the skull with icing and decorations.

¡VIVA LOS MEXICANOS!

José Guadalupe Posada

José Guadalupe Posada (hoe-SAY gwah-dah-LOO-pay poh-SAH-thah), who lived from 1851 until 1913, was a popular printmaker, cartoonist, and social commentator. He is best known for his *calaveras* (cah-lah-VAIR-ahs), or skeleton drawings, many of which are still featured in Day of the Dead decorations.

Posada and son

Make Paper flowers

This shaggy bloom, Mexico's native marigold, couldn't be easier to make. Make a bouquet for a Day of the Dead display, or anytime you want a burst of Mexican color!

YOU WILL NEED:
- Crepe paper streamers, in yellow and green
- Scissors
- Green pipe cleaners
- White glue

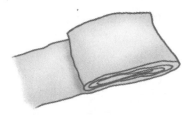

1. Cut a 4-foot (3.5-m) piece of yellow crepe paper streamer. Fold over about 2½ inches (6 cm) at one end; continue folding the paper over on itself until you reach the end. Snip through the folded edges on both sides to make a fringe. (The cuts should reach almost to the cente

2. For the flower's stem, pinch the paper in the middle. Twist one end of a pipe cleaner around the center of the paper. Fluff the paper to form a rounded blossom.

3. Cut some simple leaf shapes from green crepe paper. Glue a length of pipe cleaner — about 1 inch (2.5 cm) longer than the leaf — to the back side of each; let dry. Wrap the leaf stems to the main stem, bending the leaves to appear more natural.

¡FELIZ NAVIDAD!

For Mexicans and Christians everywhere, one of the holiest days of the year is Christmas, the birthday of Jesus Christ. As they say in Mexico, *Feliz Navidad* (fay-LEESE nah-vee-DAHD), or Happy Christmas!

For most people, the holiday season starts on December 12, the feast day of the Virgin (or Lady) of Guadalupe (see page 80). But things really get underway on the 16th of the month, when for nine nights running, families act out the journey Mary and Joseph made to Bethlehem.

Each evening, groups walk through neighborhoods by candlelight during what is called *Las Posadas*, or The Inns. Some people play the parts of Mary and Joseph (and assorted angels and shepherds); others are inside their homes acting as innkeepers. The group knocks on doors, asking for a place to spend the night. After being refused several times, they are welcomed into one of the houses, where a party takes place.

Gift-Giving

If you lived in Mexico, your family wouldn't exchange gifts on Christmas Day. Instead, you'd get presents nearly two weeks later on Epiphany (ee-PIF-an-ee), January 6. This is the day the Three Kings (or Magi, or Wise Men) presented their gifts to the baby Jesus.

Mexican children write letters to the Three Kings asking for gifts, much as many American and Canadian children write to Santa Claus. On the night of January 5, they put out hay for the Three Kings' camels and place a pair of their shoes outdoors or near a window. The next morning, the children awaken to find presents in and around the shoes.

THE GOODNIGHT FLOWER

One Mexican Christmas symbol that has made its way north — and well beyond — is the poinsettia (poyn-SET-ee-ah) plant, *La Flor de Noche Buena,* or The Christmas Eve Flower.

According to Mexican legend, the poinsettia plant came to be linked with Christmas when a poor boy knelt at the altar of his village church on Christmas Eve, wishing he had something to offer the Christ Child on His birthday. Miraculously, a poinsettia sprang up at the boy's feet. From that day forward, the colorful plant became an important symbol of Christmas.

Looking Ahead

As you've seen, Mexico is a place where the past and present are tightly interwoven. Ancient rituals and crafts are very much alive in a nation that claims the largest city on Earth.

But what does the future hold for this fascinating country and its people? If the last few decades tell us anything, Mexico can look forward to some good years, as well as some difficult times.

In recent years, the country has experienced prosperity due to the exporting of oil, manufactured goods, and food. But, many Mexicans still cannot find jobs, and the millions of people who make very little money have gotten even poorer. (Over three million people cross into the United States illegally each year to work. Most send the money they make to family members back home in Mexico.) Good times will certainly continue for some, while it will be a struggle for many others.

TRADING PARTNER

In recent years, Mexico has become an important player in global commerce. Oil and natural gas are both exported from Mexico. (Mexico has more oil and natural gas in reserve than any other country in the world, except Saudi Arabia.) Mexico is the world's leading silver producer; it also manufactures many goods and grows great quantities of food for export. The beautiful country itself is a major destination for vacationers. In fact, tourism is so important to the Mexican economy that nearly one million people work at jobs that serve only tourists!

¡VIVA LOS MEXICANOS!

Rosario Castellanos

Chiapas, a state in southern Mexico, has been the sight of violent uprisings in the 1990s by Mexican Indians who are angry about Mexico's ongoing economic and social inequalities. Rosario Castellanos knew personally about such problems in Chiapas, having seen all three classes of the Mexican people — the rich, the middle class, and the poor. (She was quite wealthy, but lived among the poor Chiapanecan Indians.)

Castellanos felt that all Mexicans, including women and Indians, must never forget the oppression they'd suffered, in order to always understand the need to search for a better tomorrow. As Castellanos wrote in one poem, *"Recuerdo, recordamos, hasta que justicia se siente entre nosotros."*

> *"I remember,*
> *let us all remember,*
> *until justice takes its place among us."*

"I need a vacation."

Visit Acapulco!

¡VIVA LOS MEXICANOS!

Carlos Fuentes

Like many 20th-century Mexicans, Carlos Fuentes became very concerned with the idea of finding and celebrating Mexico's identity: What was the true nature of Mexico, made up of so many different peoples and facing so many problems? This question was especially important in the 1940s and 1950s, when Fuentes was a young man, because the Mexican economy and society were changing so quickly. As Mexico took its place among the modern nations of the world, what would happen to its special traditions and sense of history?

Fuentes's first novel, *Where the Air Is Clean,* is about the issue of Mexico's identity. As one of the characters in that book says, "We stand at a crossroad. Which, of all roads, shall we choose?" In many ways, these words written by Carlos Fuentes in the 1950s still describe Mexico today.

HOME IS WHERE THE HEART IS

Millions of Mexicans and people of Mexican descent also make their home in the United States (and, to a lesser extent, Canada). They have kept many of their homeland's customs alive, and each year share them with friends and neighbors throughout North America.

You can learn a lot from the Mexican kids in your area. Ask a friend what her name means in English; trade part of your bag lunch with someone who brings authentic Mexican food for lunch each day. Practice speaking Spanish with boys and girls who are native speakers.

As you learn about Mexican customs and culture, be sure to share some of your family's traditions with your new friends.

AMERICANS ALL

Many Mexicans refer to themselves as *americanos,* or Americans. After all, Mexico is part of the Americas. So what do they call people who live in the United States and Canada? *Norteamericanos,* or North Americans!

¡Adiós Amigos!

RESOURCES

Bonifaz, Oscar. *Remembering Rosario: A Personal Glimpse into the Life and Works of Rosario Castellanos.* Scripta Humanistica, 1990.

Coe, Michael D. *America's First Civilization: Discovering the Olmec.* American Heritage Publishing Co., 1968.

Coe, Michael D., Dean Snow, and Elizabeth Benson. *Atlas of Ancient America.* Facts on File Publications, 1986.

de Beer, Gabriella. *Contemporary Mexican Women Writers.* University of Texas Press, 1996.

Faris, Wendy B. *Carlos Fuentes.* Frederick Ungar Publishing Co., 1983.

Foster, Lynn V. *A Brief History of Mexico.* Facts on File, Inc., 1997.

Greene, Jacqueline Dembar. *The Maya.* Franklin Watts, 1992.

Haskins, Jim. *Count Your Way Through Mexico.* Carolrhoda Books, 1989.

Kalman, Bobbie. *Mexico: The Culture.* Crabtree Publishing, 1993.

Kalman, Bobbie. *Mexico: The People.* Crabtree Publishing, 1993.

Kent, Deborah. *Mexico: Rich in Spirit and Tradition.* Marshall Cavendish, 1996.

Kismaric, Susan. *Manuel Alvarez Bravo.* Museum of Modern Art, New York, 1997.

Krupp, Robin Rector. *Let's Go Traveling in Mexico.* Morrow Junior Books, 1996.

Morley, Sylvanus Griswold. *The Ancient Maya,* 3rd Edition. Stanford University Press, 1956.

Nuñez, Marco. Consulate General of Mexico.

Rosenbloom, Morris. *Heroes of Mexico.* Fleet Press Corp., 1969.

Salinas-Norman, Bobbi. *Indo-Hispanic Folk Art Traditions, I and II.* Piñata Publications, 1988.

Shalant, Phyllis. *Look What We've Brought You From Mexico.* Julian Messner, 1992.

Temko, Florence. *Traditional Crafts from Mexico and Central America.* Lerner Publications, 1996.

Williams, Raymond Leslie. *The Writings of Carlos Fuentes.* University of Austin Press, 1996.

INDEX